EXCEL PIVOTTABLES
AND
DASHBOARD

The Step-By-Step Guide to Learn and Master Excel PivotTables and Dashboard

HEIN SMITH

TABLE OF CONTENTS

Introduction 1

   Overview: Best Use of and Practice 3

Chapter 1: Version Compatibility 9

   Backward Compatibility.. 9

   Licensing: Subscription versus Perpetual 16

Chapter 2: Basic PivotTable Functions........................18

   Office 365 Excel 2019 Build Features and Functionality.............. 19

   Enabling Power Pivot Add-in: New Pivot Table Controls on the
Desktop Version 26

   Implementing Your First PivotTable.............................. 31

   Control PivotTables Using New PivotTable Defaults.................... 36

   Excel for the Web: Share your PivotTables with Colleagues......... 48

Chapter 3: Automation and Efficiency...........................58

   Shortcuts and Tips 59

   Automate PivotTables with Macros in VBA 71

Chapter 4: Analysis...95

   Overview: Process of Analysis 96

   Providing Context: Creating and Managing Multiple Pivot Tables97

   Creating: Discovering and Validating New Perspectives
on the Data 103

Chapter 5: Investigative Modeling using Pivot Charts 105

    Principals in Data Modeling 106

    Creating Visualizations... 112

    Interpreting Data using Visualizations........................ 114

Chapter 6: Troubleshooting 118

    Power Pivot Ribbon Disappears.................................. 118

    Problems with Adding Slicers...................................... 128

Conclusion...132

Reference...135

Introduction

Welcome to the Excel PivotTables and Dashboard mastery guide! This e-book is intended for freelancers who have been asked to implement analyses and consultants who help inform decision-makers. This book will empower you, as the data person, to separate yourself from others in your field by incorporating additional value to your services through making adaptive reports. This book is also both for the Excel aficionado and the intermediate Excel user who wants to get more functionality out of their Microsoft Excel product. Regardless, the goal is to allow you to stay ahead of the other Excel power users with a sleek resource and reference for your skills.

That being said, foremost, this book is a resource for mastering easy, powerful techniques to create, customize, change, and control PivotTables in Excel. As you encounter analysis problems, you may return to this book to help strategize your approach. This book also features some common troubleshooting issues to get you started on solving technical issues.

To begin, let's discuss a quick definition of PivotTables. PivotTables are a collection of built-in tools that Excel uses to compile more comprehensible reports from spreadsheet data, including data from various Excel files. PivotTable tools filter, sort, rearrange, and calculate data to summarize databases.

These PivotTable features allow you to extract specific information into reports, which can facilitate better explorations of trends in data and predictive features. How you extract and extrapolate this data, of course, depends on the purposes of the report. As with any tool PivotTables ultimately only allows you to visualize data in different ways. How these visualizations are interpreted and the conclusions reached depend on the analytical know-how of the analyst.

Expanding the functionality of Excel depends solely on the version of Excel of your client or employer. This includes PivotTables and the functions used within them. Excel 2019 has added more PivotTable features that may not be backwards compatible to an older perpetual license. This is important for freelancers and consultants because these features may not be viewable on the client's native desktop versions of Excel. This lack of backwards compatibility also makes it difficult to recreate and execute newer features on older versions of Excel. Ergo, it is important when conducting your data dissections and compilations on Excel 2019 or Office 365. Reports are always viewable on Microsoft's office live online Excel client.

To begin, let us start with an overview of the purpose and the best uses of this text. The next section will give an exhaustive overview of text features and how to take the best advantage of them.

Overview: Best Use of and Practice

This book is a collection of supplementary information to review before and after the illustrated demonstrations. In addition to being useful for individuals who favor additional instruction and illustration before application, this book is a superior substitute for most online tutorials. Most Excel aficionados became this way through searching for features online. This is a novel and resourceful way to learn; even this book includes the best sources for this purpose as well. However, these online tutorials are scattered and not unified. This book unifies examples and demonstrations.

Note:

Important and noteworthy information will be separated from other texts accordingly. They will be separated from the main text and can occur at any point in the book.

One useful site used to source our demonstration and references is the Microsoft Office Support site. Each demonstration will point to its associated Microsoft Excel exercises for demonstration and practice ("Create a PivotTable to analyze worksheet data," n.d.). This site is useful because it features samples and screenshots from several platforms. These platform versions include Windows (PC), Mac (iOS), and the Microsoft Live web-based platform.

One of the limitations of the Microsoft Office Support site, however, is that the demonstrations do not feature more realistic datasets. The majority of these datasets are simple examples, featuring incredibly small dimensions, i.e. 3x4 datasets with nonsense data within. While these examples serve as a way to clearly demonstrate the functions, they do not demonstrate how the function is actually used to solve problems.

Demonstrations with a Large Dataset

This book will also feature demonstrations using this large, 6370x17 dataset for practice:

http://www3.wabash.edu/econometrics/EconometricsBook/Chapters/Ch03PivotTables/ExcelFiles/EastNorthCentralFTWorkers.xls

This public workbook file was originally crafted for an introductory econometrics course. Specifically, the dataset was created for their chapter covering pivottables ("Introductory Econometrics Chapter 3: Pivot Tables," n.d.). Econometrics itself involves large demographical datasets. PivotTables require continuous data, i.e. data with no empty rows or columns interspersed in between ("Create a PivotTable to analyze worksheet data," n.d.). Therefore, to create this dataset, the census data had to be cleaned and formatted properly for demonstrations. This serves our purpose because it makes a comprehensible yet large enough dataset to demonstrate the power of pivot tables.

For the purpose of our demonstrations, we will be focusing on these specific workbook dataset features:

- Raw "Data" sheet for performing exercises

- Named Ranges for large dataset management

- Summary of stats generated by Excel's Data Analysis add-in

- 6366 individuals with 17 different measured variables

- "Q&A" sheet with simple contextual exercises

This large dataset will be used to demonstrate features on a more complex table, which is closer to what you might be using these features for in the wild. As an effect, you will also be guided through real world troubleshooting and limitations for these functions.

Note:

Demonstration portions are linked to their associated troubleshooting items in chapter 7

Project Flowthrough: Best approach to a project

With an understanding of the main features of the book, we can move on to discussing an overview of topics. This book follows the logical steps from getting started, such as a review of basic functions, to analysis, and the finalization process for a report. The basic flowthrough of the book can be summarized as follows:

(1) Version Considerations and Compatibility

(2) Basic functions

(3) Automation

(4) Analysis

(5) Modeling

(6) Reporting and Sharing

Note:

Instructions on how to navigate the platform will be given in path form. Using the flowthrough process of the book listed above, in path form it would be:

Version Considerations and

CompatibilityBasic functions > Automation >...

...Analysis > Modeling > Reporting and Sharing

With "Reporting and Sharing" being the final step in the instructional path.

Version considerations and compatibility will cover Excel 2019 and Office 365 extensively. It will also overview limitations of previous, "perpetual" licenses. Understanding version considerations and compatibility is important for getting started and for troubleshooting software issues. This book will also discuss meeting and anticipating often "unspoken project requirements" for freelancers. Most of these issues occur in this section, but will be detailed throughout the book in verison considerations.

While this book is intended for both power users and users looking to expand their knowledge of Excel, this book will still review basic functions. Expertise begins with a grasp of fundamentals, and even the savviest expert can learn new basic functions. This section will help you familiarize yourself with the platform. All functions will be labeled for version compatibility.

Basic functions will continue over to the automation and efficiency section. This section will include ways of automating some basic functions in order to establish more efficient workflows. Similar to the previous section, power users may benefit the most from this section, including implementing macros using the Visual Basic (VBA) editor console.

Distinguishing itself from the wealth of tutorials available online, this book will briefly provide an overview of general principals in analysis used to qualify and quantify your data. This book was crafted for the purpose of discussing analysis, which is why the large dataset was selected for the demonstrations. The large dataset uses data pulled from a public source with dynamic values. Demonstrations using this dataset will show you how to identify trends and how to visualize them. Using these raw datasets will make it easier to discuss general principles of analysis. This book will showcase 4 basic analysis techniques to get started.

This book will also discuss modeling features and point to specific Microsoft Support Excel features used to model data. As in previous chapters, some of these features will be Excel 2019 and Office 365 specific. Some features will be backwards compatible and will only be mentioned as a method of modeling in PivotCharts.

Note:

This book will only label Excel 2016 and forward. For Excel 2013 and backwards, please refer to the Microsoft Support Excel Features.

Finally, the last chapter will focus on reporting and sharing This chapter will go into detail about Excel functions and PivotTable features that allow you to transform huge data sets into clear summary reports. As the final step in the process it will encapsulate the previous steps such as modeling and contextual aspects of analysis. This chapter will also go into detail vehicles of sharing your analysis and best practices.

Chapter 1

Version Compatibility

Backward Compatibility

Note:

If you are developing a solution for a client, inquire about your client's version of Excel. Make sure that your sheet will work on their version of Excel; especially so if they are using an older version of Excel.

Google Sheets is a popular product for spreadsheets among entrepreneurs. However, Google Sheets is not fully transferable to Excel.

Backwards compatibility is critical for troubleshooting sheet problems. Backwards compatibility is the ability of a piece of software to interact with previous versions. Microsoft files are backwards compatible, meaning that an *Excel 2013 file* will work on a newer, 2019, Office 365 version of Excel. However, an unmodified 2019 Office 365 file will not be able to work well on a 2013 version of Excel. The Office 365 file will have to be modified to work on the 2013 build of Excel. This can be done through saving the Office 365 file as an 2013 Excel file. This solution can be less than ideal because 2013 Excel files are restricted to only Excel 2013 formulas and features. The majority of the PivotTable features and functions covered in this text are from the latest Excel 2019 build. Therefore, a 2019, Office 365 file with PivotTables and extensive reporting will not be able to work on an Excel 2013 build.

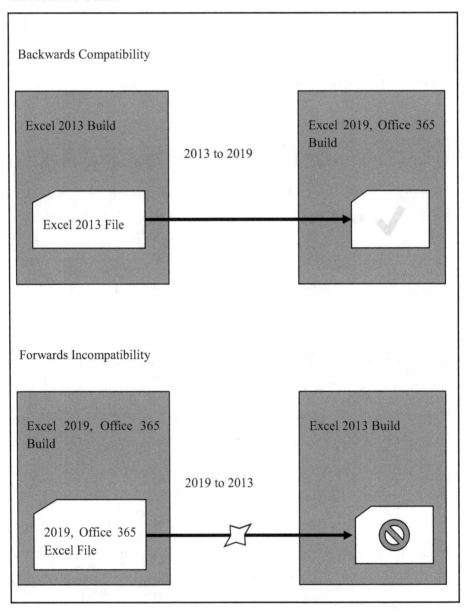

File Behavior for Microsoft Office Excel: Backwards Compatibility and Forwards Incompatibility

This diagram depicts how different builds of Microsoft Excel builds interact with each other. A "build" is a term that describes a specific version of software. Microsoft practices backwards compatibility, which means that more recent builds will always be able to accept older versions of files. This is illustrated by the top half of the diagram.

However, newer files will not be able to run on older builds. This "Forwards Incompatibility" is depicted by the lower half of the diagram. Microsoft practices forwards incompatibility in order to encourage people still using old builds to update to the latest software for new features.

Note: In Excel, "files" are also known as "workbooks." They are called workbooks because each file can have numerous sheets stored within them. This is a reference to accountants who kept their physical spreadsheets in workbook binders. This distinction becomes important in the automation chapter when you start consolidating different workbooks and sheets. You will need to know the difference in order to instruct Excel properly.

Knowing how backwards compatibility works will inadvertently save you many hours of back and forth. For example, let's say you are a freelancer who developed an Excel sheet that calculates and reports summaries of your client's data. You used your subscription licensed, Office 365 version of Excel.

Your client downloads the sheet to install it into their outfit, but then reports that the product you provided for them is *totally inoperable.* How might you begin troubleshooting? The very first step is to determine what version of Excel your client is using. If you know that your client is trying to use a 2013 copy of Excel, the Office 365 sheet is unable to run on Excel 2013. While you can convert the file to Excel 2013, you may lose the very functionality that the client needed the Excel file to do.

Newer functions are not supported in older software builds of Excel. This forwards incompatibility is embedded into Microsoft's software model as a means to encourage businesses to update to the latest build to take advantage of the newer, and usually more powerful, builds. Returning to our example, you still may have some options depending on the sorts of features of the sheet. If your client only needs to view the results of reports, you may be able to share the sheet using the Microsoft Live, web platform version of Excel. We'll discuss how to share sheets using the web platform with more specific examples and functionality in later chapters.

How to Check Your Version of Excel

For now, Microsoft has a backward compatibility scheme: newer versions of Excel will always be able to load and render old Excel files, while older versions of Excel cannot handle new Excel file sheets. To begin troubleshooting this issue, you need to check the license of your Excel.

File>Account Screen for Office 365 Excel

The target screen depicting account information. In addition to account information such as the email associated with Microsoft Office Online Live, if you have one, it also shows the current version of your Office products.

For this text, we will be using an Office 365 subscription product. Excel 2019 perpetual license builds will have a slightly different screen.

To access the build and version of your Excel, perform the following steps:

1. Open up a new or existing document to gain access to the main menu

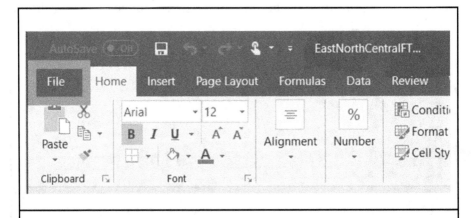

Excel Main Menu

This menu is only accessible when you open up an excel file. This view features the "Home" ribbon that opens as the default upon opening a file.

2. *File > Account*, which produces the "Product Information" page

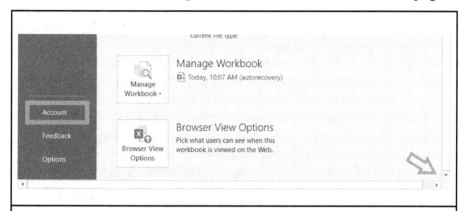

"Account" Location

Be sure to scroll down the Excel: File screen to access the File>Account screen. The Excel: File main screen was designed to be an aggregate of information. There is a lot of information here about the file and other files on your computer in some cases. You will have to scroll down and navigate through to find the items you need.

Note:

You can use "*File > Account...*" on Excel 2016 and later.

Please remember that *only* 2016 and forward build functions and features will be labeled. While this book may discuss features from 2013, they will not be labeled accordingly since they will work on all modern builds of Excel.

The "Product Information" page allows you to see the license, who the license belongs to, and the current version.

Licensing: Subscription versus Perpetual

Microsoft has two licensing schemes: subscription and perpetual licenses. Due to the nature of perpetual licenses, if you have one, you will constantly have to check your copy of Excel and compare it to the latest Excel. Perpetual licenses, as the name suggests, is software that you own the license to forever. These licenses are sufficient for home and student versions of Microsoft software. These licenses are sometimes included with the purchase of a Microsoft Windows laptop computer. This can be a feasible way to purchase Microsoft Office software as the average lifespan of a PC is around 3 to 5 years (Koble, n.d.).

However, one drawback of a perpetual license is that they do not get updated with new features. This may be fine with software like Microsoft Word or Powerpoint. In contrast to other items in the suite, Microsoft Excel is constantly getting upgraded through suggestions of beta test users ("Microsoft wants you to beta test upcoming Office products and services | Windows Central," n.d.). Power users and beta testers will then purchase a subscription-based license. A subscription-based license means that your product will be upgraded with every new release. Microsoft offers its subscription software in a software suite marketed as "Office 365". In the year that this text is composed, both Office 365 and Excel 2019 have the same features. The only difference between them in the current year is that the Excel 2019 refers to a 2019 build under a perpetual license. This current build will be referred to as the Excel 2019, Office 365 build.

Independently, Office 365 requires that you must pay a yearly fee. Subscriptions can become more expensive than the perpetual licenses since new features are only released every 3 years or so. However, Microsoft manages the software updates for you so that you don't have to update your software every three years. There are also other features offered in the Office 365 subscription license that benefits power users, but this text will only focus on PivotTables and other features that make them a powerful analysis tool.

As mentioned before, old features used in the analysis and demonstrations are backward compatible to the Excel 2019, Office 365 build. These older features are also more friendly to old perpetual licenses. As such, in this text, only newer features will be labeled accordingly.

Note

The Microsoft Office Support site labels older versions from 2013 and forward to help mitigate "forwards incompatibility". However, this is not a concern with an Office 365 subscription.

Chapter 2

Basic PivotTable Functions

When discussing software and how it can help us achieve a result, it is important to know the difference between software features and software functionality. Software features are a list of tasks that the software can do. Excel essentially is an extensive calculator that calculates items in real time cell by cell. It uses various functions to achieve certain things, but these functions are just another feature of the program.

Functionality, however, is how a feature can be utilized to achieve a certain result. We want Excel to produce certain deliverables for us, such as reports on a given data set. Features like pivot tables, functions, and slicers allow us to achieve the goal, but using these features is not the end goal.

Stepping back for a moment, the end goal of this text is to use these features in order to learn them. From this perspective, this makes the concept of "functionality" ubiquitous. In other words, while learning aspects of Excel, it may be difficult to grasp the concept of functionality right away because the end goal is to explore features.

It is important to set this distinction between features versus functionality because it will help you deploy Excel in more savvy ways. An Excel power user is not valuable for their knowledge of Excel features. The power user is valuable because they know how to utilize those features to solve any problem presented to them.

To overcome this instructional obscurity between features and functionality, this book deploys examples with a "theoretical goal". Specifically, each demonstration will detail the situational functionality of the feature through providing an example. In this chapter, we will begin by covering new Excel 2019 formulas can be used in calculating items within the pivot table.

Office 365 Excel 2019 Build Features and Functionality

As previously discussed, specific Office 365 Excel 2019 functions and features are not compatible with older builds due to forwards incompatibility. Ergo, Excel files that use specific Office 365 Excel 2019 features will not be able to run on older builds. These Excel 2019 files can still be viewed on Microsoft Office live online web client. We'll discuss sharing and viewing files in detail in later chapters.

These formula functions are important for calculations within pivot tables. Formulas are functions that are called using the "=" sign that allow you to do calculations and other data manipulations. Each function has a specific syntax, or a programmed configuration where you enter operands for the function to operate on. They can also be used as expressions. Expressions are formulas that test if a given condition is true.

Note:

The Microsoft Office Support site has a living catalogue of functions with their build labeled. As of this writing, they only have Office 365 until 2010 labeled, with no 2019. It can be assumed that Office 365 labeled formulas will eventually be categorized as Excel 2019 once the Office Support website updates. You can view the catalogue at their website.

Here are some examples of new Office 365 Excel 2019 functions:

IFS (Office Excel 2019, Excel for Web)

In the past, to test conditions for several scenarios, you had to write a complicated nested IF formula. This new formula allows you to run several logical tests as well as specify the value of each test if the test is true ("IFS function," n.d.).

Here is the syntax for the $IFS()$ formula:

$$IFS(logical\_test1, value\_if\_true1, [logical\_test2, value\_if\_true2],,...)$$

While this function can take up to 127 arguments, the purpose of the function was to reduce large logical nested formulas. Creating a large IFS train of logical tests defeats this purpose. For responsive sheets where data is constantly changing, a $SWITCH()$ function may be more appropriate.

This function is accompanied by *MINIFS()*, *MAXIFS()*, *SUMIFS()*, *AVERAGEIFS()*, and *COUNTIFS()*. These functions can also be used on Excel's web platform. These are functions that allow you to apply some calculation when some conditions are met, where:

MINIFS(): When given several ranges, returns the minimum value among them specified by a multiple expressions

MAXIFS(): When given several ranges, returns the maximum value among them specified by multiple expressions.

SUMIFS(): Function within the math and trig functions that, when given several ranges, returns the sum of values among them specified by multiple expressions.

AVERAGEIFS(): When given several ranges, returns the arithmetic mean among them that meet multiple specified criteria.

COUNTIFS(): When given several ranges, counts each cell that meets multiple specified criteria. This function also uses arguments such as the question mark (?) and the asterisk (*).

For example, consider our large dataset and the function *COUNTIFS()*.

[Demonstration, pivot table count if greater than a certain percentage. Purpose is to identify ways of segmenting the dataset that is more meaningful. Not helpful, for example, to look at people who make more than $150k because there are so few in the dataset.]

Recall our discussion about functionality: using features and functions to achieve a specific result. As we have learned, the takeaway is that the advanced IFS functions applies various calculations on ranges based on multiple expressions. This reduces nested arguments to achieve a specific result. However, the IFS functions are better suited for decision making formulas, i.e. calculate the data in this way when a condition is met. For dynamic sheets that have constantly changing data, utilizing a pivottable with a $SWITCH()$ may be more appropriate.

SWITCH (Office Excel 2019, Excel for Web)

In programming, switch functions are used to control the operations of program using a single expression. In Excel, the $SWITCH()$ formula would be used to display a specific result based on the data provided. This is helpful for creating dynamic and adaptable pivottables and reports. Therefore, the $SWITCH()$ function is very useful for automating reports, which we will talk about at length in the next chapter.

Here is the syntax for the $SWITCH()$ formula:

$$SWITCH(expression, value1, result1, [default\ or\ value2, result2],$$

$$...[default\ or\ value3, result3])$$

This function evaluates an expression against a list of values and returns an indicated result ("SWITCH function," n.d.).

Other Office 365 Excel 2019 Functions

The various $IFS()$ functions and $SWITCH()$ add more functionality to Excel for analysis and modeling in particular, allowing you to seamlessly add more automated decision making to your sheets. These functions are the most powerful in pivottables because they allow you to call on and calculate data more seamlessly then in previous Excel builds.

Some other functions introduced in Excel 2019 were designed to make text handling easier. $CONCAT()$ is an updated version of the old $CONCATENATE()$ function. This function has the following syntax:

$$CONCAT(text1, [text2], ...)$$

It allows you to combine strings of text from various ranges, however, it does not include the delimiter. For example the formula:

$$= CONCAT("The", "quick", "brown", "fox",$$
$$"jumped", "over", "the", "lazy", "dog.")$$

Would produce:

$$Thequick\mathbf{brownfoxjumpsoverthelazydog}.$$

In previous builds of Excel, in order to handle text, delimiters had to be added manually. Microsoft developed $TEXTJOIN()$ for Excel 2019 to add delimiters more quickly. The syntax for $TEXTJOIN()$ is as follows:

$$TEXTJOIN(delimiter, ignore\_empty, text1, [text2], ...)$$

The *ignore_empty* argument is required and indicates whether or not you want the function to ignore empty cells. This is particularly important when using $TEXTJOIN()$ to join a range of cells. Returning to our previous example, we can make the phrase more readable by indicating a delimiter.

$$= TEXTJOIN(" ", "TRUE", "The", "quick", "brown", "fox",$$

$$"jumped", "over", "the", "lazy", "dog.")$$

Would produce:

The quick **brown fox jumps over the lazy dog**.

Returning to our conversation about functionality, these text handling functions are useful for automating labeling in PivotTables. Charts and tables must be labeled accurately. Using $CONCAT()$, or $TEXTJOIN()$ for longer complicated ranges of text, allows you to also automate labeling. We will also discuss best modeling and data reporting practices in later chapters.

Forecasting Functions (Office 365 Excel 2019, 2016)

One powerful feature of excel is using historical data to predict future values. Forecasting functions are used to predict future values ("Forecasting functions (reference)," n.d.). There are several functions that use different algorithms for different applications:

FORECAST.ETS(): Function that predicts a single future value given historical data using the AAA version of the Exponential Smoothing (ETS) algorithm.

FORECAST.ETS.SEASONALITY(): Function that returns a repetitive pattern Excel detects from a specified time series when given historical data using the ETS algorithm.

FORECAST.LINEAR(): Function that predicts a single future value given an independent value and historical data using linear (X,Y) regression. Independent values usually occur in units of time.

FORECAST.ETS.CONFINT() : Function that returns a confidence interval for a forecast value at a specified target date given historical data.

FORECAST.ETS.STAT(): Function that returns one of eight statistical parameters, metrics, or step sizes given historical data. You can learn more about the statistical parameters available for this function at the Microsoft Office Support website ("FORECAST.ETS.STAT function," n.d.).

This has applications in the financial sector for predicting the sales price of products or consumer trends. These functions can also be used to mathematically investigate confidence level and statistical aspects such as data aggregation step size, how the data collasacques into steps. As of now, these functions seem to only be available to Office 365 subscribers. However, the forecast functions are available in Excel web version.

Generally, all the new Excel 2019 formulas simplify certain computations including tasks that would have required nested functions and text handling. The forecast functions are powerful functions that give you access to data prediction and statistics. However, as we discussed, relying on these new formulas for computations will make it difficult to view in older versions of Excel.

Note:

New formulas can still be viewed in the web version. This can be a work around solution for clients with older, perpetual licenses. However, these formulas can only be edited or manipulated with desktop build of Office 365 Excel 2019.

These functions can be deployed inside of PivotTables to control the content of the widgets. Most PivotTable controls can only be viewed in the web version. To implement the pivottables you need a desktop build of Excel.

Enabling Power Pivot Add-in: New Pivot Table Controls on the Desktop Version

Power pivot is the PivotTable wizard for analysis. It is only available for Office 365 subscription licenses, the 2019 perpetual licenses, and the professional plus perpetual licenses ("Where is Power Pivot?," n.d.). It is only available on Windows. You also need to have these desktop versions to use the wizard, however, it is not enabled by default.

To enable Power Pivot for the first time you must initialize the Power Pivot add-in. To do this you must ("Start the Power Pivot add-in for Excel," n.d.):

Note:

Power Pivot is only available on Windows builds of Excel, including Office 365 subscription products. As of this writing, Mac users do not have access to the Power Pivot add-in.

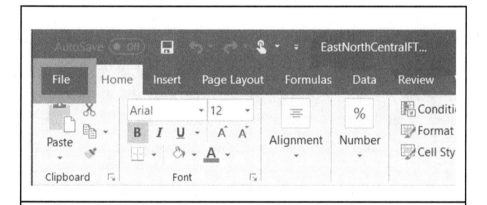

Excel Main Menu

This menu is only accessible when you open up an Excel file.

1. Go to *File* > *Options* > *Add* − *Ins.*

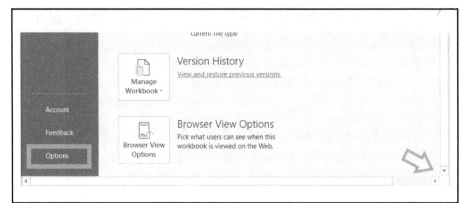

"Options" Location

Be sure to scroll down the Excel: File screen to access the File>Options screen. The Excel: File main screen was designed to be an aggregate of information, therefore, there is a lot of information here about the file and other files on your computer in some cases. This can make it difficult to find the information you need.

You will have to scroll down and navigate to the Options button to access the options window.

2. In the **Managage** box, navigate to *COM Add − ins > Go.*

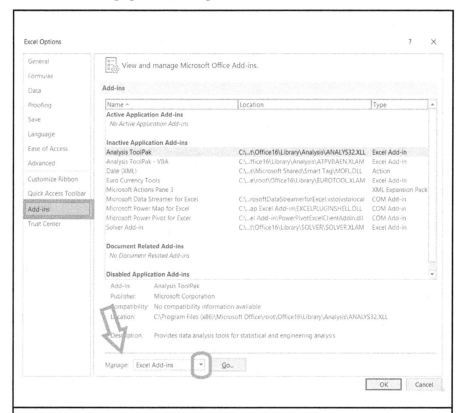

"Add-ins" Dialogue Window

Clicking "Options" will close the Excel: File window and open a separate dialogue window entitled "Excel Options". To access the Excel Options: Add-ins window, you must navigate the menu to the left. The "Manage" box is a drop-down menu at the bottom of the dialogue window. This image shows what appears in the Manage drop-down menu upon opening the window. Click the downward triangle (▼) box to navigate to *COM Add − ins* and click "Go" to access the COM Add-ins dialogue window.

3. Check the Microsoft Office Power Pivot box and click OK.

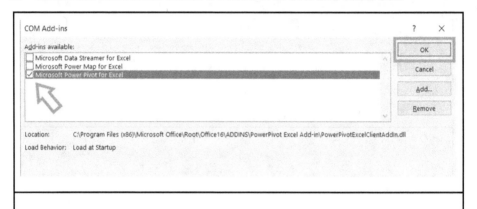

"COM Add-ins" Dialogue Window

Clicking "Go" will close the Excel Options: Add-ins window and open a separate dialogue window entitled "COM Add-ins". Toggle the "Microsoft Office Power Pivot" box and click OK. This will instantly add "Power Pivot" to your main menu ribbon.

Now you will be able to access the Power Pivot add-in from the main menu ribbon:

Excel Main Menu with the Power Pivot Ribbon

Clicking "OK" will close the "COM Add-ins" box and instantly ad the Power Pivot Ribbon. These items are disabled until you generate and select pivottables to manage.

To maintain performance, Excel is programmed to refresh itself if there is a problem with the program. As a result, all Add-ins may disappear. Specifically, this may cause your Power Pivot ribbon to disappear if Excel closes unexpectedly while the Power Pivot window is opened. Restoring Power Pivot to the menu is covered in the troubleshooting section.

Implementing Your First PivotTable

Looking at the Power Pivot ribbon, you will notice that the features are disabled. You must have at least one PivotTable for it to be activated. For many of the features, you must have several PivotTables to make the most out of Power Pivot features. Let's start with creating and building a PivotTable of average usual hours worked by sex.

1. Select the "Recorded Variables" section of the table

File	Home	Insert	Page Layout	**Formulas**	Data	Review	View	Help	Power Pivot

fx Insert Function — ∑ AutoSum ⌄, Recently Used ⌄, Financial ⌄ — Logical ⌄, Text ⌄, Date & Time ⌄ — Defined Names ⌄ — Trace Precedents, Trace Dependents, Remove Arrows ⌄

Function Library — Formula Auditing

A3 · ⋮ × ✓ fx Recoded Variables

	A	B	C	D	E	F	G	H	I
2	6366 full-time workers in five North-Central States, March 1999								
3				Recoded Variables					
4	Usual Hours Worked	Education (yrs)	Yearly Earnings	Race	Sex	Usual Weekly Earnings	State	Month in Sample	A_GRSWK
5	40	13	$ 44,000	White	Male	$ 858	Ohio	8	858
6	35	12	$ 12,000	White	Female	.	Ohio	3	0
7	70	11	$ 54,000	White	Male	.	Ohio	3	0
8	40	16	$ 48,200	White	Male	.	Ohio	7	0
9	38	12	$ 24,000	White	Male	.	Ohio	2	0
10	60	18	$ 62,000	White	Female	.	Ohio	5	0

Using Keyboard shortcuts to select Recorded Variables: A3:H6370

There are over 6,000 rows. The fastest way to manage a dataset this large is using keyboard shortcuts and the features of the table. Cell A3 spans the section of "Recorded Variables". Select A3, tap the $[Down - Arrow]$key, and then press:

$[CTRL] + [SHIFT] + [END]$

This selects the whole table. To isolate the selection to the Recorded Variables, hold:

$[SHIFT] + [Left - Arrow]$

It will automatically accept the bounds of Recorded Variables. This saves time in scrolling.

Note:

Creating a named range here is helpful for reducing table scrolling time. A "named range" is a variable you can set in Excel that stands for a range. This sheet already has a "Recorded_Variables" range, but it does not include our target rows and columns. To create a correct range, once you've selected our target range go to:

$Formulas > Defined\ Names > "New"$

A dialogue box will pop up. Name it "Pivot_Table_Values" and it should refer to:

$$= Data!\ \$A\$3: \$H\$6370$$

2. Go to *Insert > "Tables" drop – down > PivotTable*

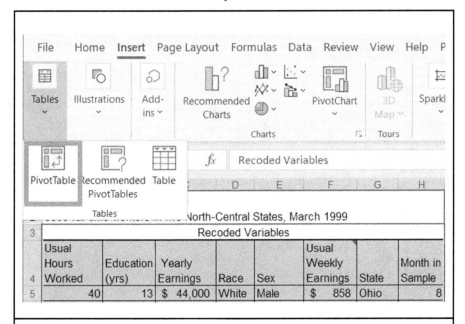

Office 365 Excel 2019 New Layout: Insert>Tables Drop-down Menu

Excel 2019 has a different layout to access PivotTables. This may be jarring to users on older perpetual licenses, or anyone using Microsoft Support Online's general instructions. PivotTables are consolidated with the other tables in a "Tables" section.

3. Create the new PivotTable in Summary Stats

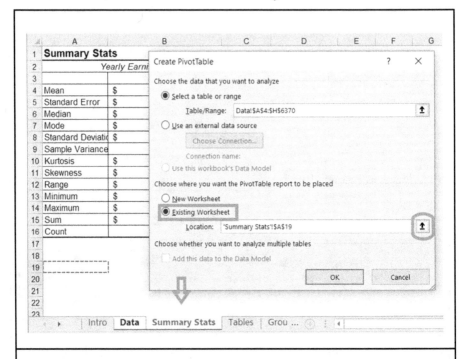

Create PivotTable Dialogue on Summary Stats Sheet

We are placing our first pivottable on the Summary Stats Sheet to in order to keep all of our stats in one place. To access this (1) click on "Existing Worksheet" and (2) in the "Location" box, click the up-arrow icon. This allows you to navigate the workbook. (3) Navigate to the "Summary Stats" sheet and select one of the cells.

If you would like a shortcut, after selecting "Existing Worksheet" you can paste $'Summary\ Stats'!\$A\$19$ into the "Location" box. Hit OK.

4. Build the Pivot Table with the following: Average of Usual Hours Worked and Sex

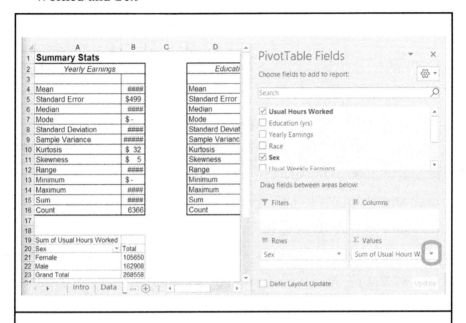

Create Average of Usual Hours Worked and Sex

After selecting "Usual Hours Worked" and "Sex", Excel automatically populates which value should be in the rows and which should be used for the calculated varaibles. It also automatically populates the pivottable with the calculated sums. However, we want the *Average of Usual Hours worked*. To get the Average of Usual Hours worked, click on the down arrow highlighted above and select "Average".

5. Save the current work

> **Note:**
>
> Using $[CTRL] + [S]$ is the safest way to save your work. This is because navigating through the graphical user interface (GUI) features such as the Excel:File window can cause hiccups. This is especially true in resource intensive programs like most Microsoft products, given our experience with the Excel:File interface. Using keyboard shortcuts to save your files reduces computations in the program, thus decreasing the risk of program crashes. To access "Save As" use $[F12]$ or $[fn] + [F12]$ on some newer laptops. This opens a less intensive save-as prompt window.

We will be using this pivottable to demonstrate the Excel 2019 controls in the next chapter.

Control PivotTables Using New PivotTable Defaults

The EastNorthCentralFTWorkers workbook has a Q&A at the end of the book that includes some exercises and demonstrations for the course. These exercises and demonstrations are, of course, specific to the econometrics course. One example is the stark difference between the total average of usual hours worked and the simple average. These are statistic questions that we will not focus on here, but we will create a bar graph showing the demographical data in later chapters.

This chapter will focus on how to manipulate the data on the fly using the pivot table fields. Our first PivotTable entitled "Average of Usual Hours Worked" only has two variables. Let's begin by creating another, more dynamic pivot table called "Average Yearly Earnings broken down by Sex and Education." The steps will be similar to the previous section.

Building a Pivot Table using Drag and Drop Features

1. Select the "Recorded Variables" section of the table

		Clipboard		Font			

| able_Value ▼ | : | ✕ | ✓ | fx | Recoded Variables | | |

	B	C	D	E	F
Education		Recoded Variables			
EducRecode					
GMSTCENtoSt..				Usual	
HGAtoEduc	ducation	Yearly			Weekly	
Intercept	yrs)	Earnings	Race	Sex	Earnings	St
	12	$ 44,000	White	Male	$ 858	O
Pivot_Table_V.	12	$ 12,000	White	Female	.	O
Recoded_Vari..	11	$ 54,000	White	Male	.	O
Slope	16	$ 48,200	White	Male	.	O
Usual_Hours_..	12	$ 24,000	White	Male	.	O
10	60	18	$ 62.000	White	Female	.	O

Using Named Ranges in Office 365 Excel 2019

If you named your range "Pivot_Table_Values" in the first demonstration, you should be able to select the range by using this drop down box to the left of the formula bar. Using this drop down bar automatically selects the named range for you.

The down arrow was added in this screenshot to help you with the location of the dropdown. This arrow disappears when the drop-down menu is activated.

2. Go to *Insert > "Tables" drop − down > PivotTable*

3. Create the new PivotTable in Summary Stats

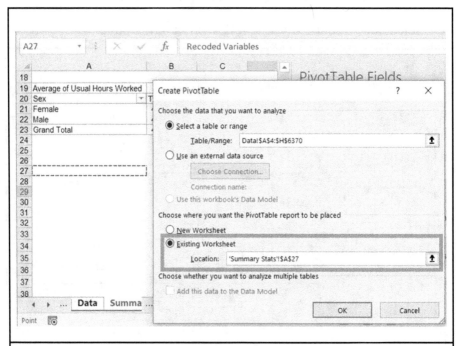

Creating an Additional PivotTable

We will be creating the additional pivottable on the Summary Stats sheet underneath the first one. Click "Existing Worksheet" and copy the following expression into the Location box:

$$'Summary\ Stats'! \$A\$27$$

4. Build the Pivot Table with the following: Average Yearly Earnings broken down by Education in the rows and Sex in the columns

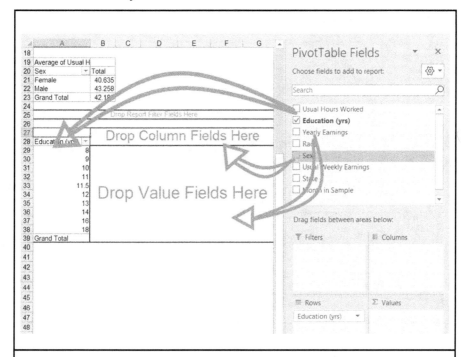

Building a PivotTable using drag-and-drop features

Office 365 Excel 2019 PivotTable defaults allow you to drag and drop fields as well. Click on the field in the list and drag them to the section you want. It is better to start with (1) rows, (2) columns and then (3) values.

5. Be sure to adjust the values to calculate the *average*.

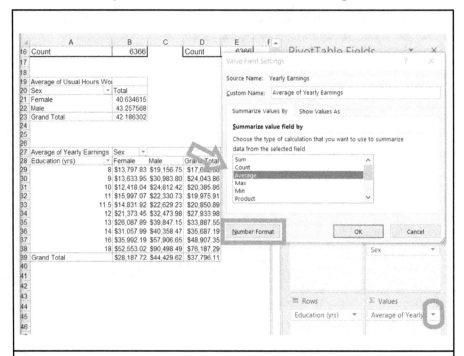

Adjusting the Values

Upon generating the table, Excel automatically calculates the various sums of each category. However, the example asks for the average. Just as before, this can be accessed in the drop down menu underneath values. As this is yearly earnings, this should be formatted as currency. Click on "Number Format" to change the numbers into dollars.

6. Save your progress

This will create an additional pivottable with more fields to explore. One additional feature that was not added were "filters." Filter fields allow you to drill down into the data. The better fields to include into the filter section would be independent variables that only have a few arguments such as State, Race, or Month in Sample. Sex, only having two arguments in this dataset, is also a good canidate for filters. You can drag these fields down to the filter section and explore how they help you segment the data further.

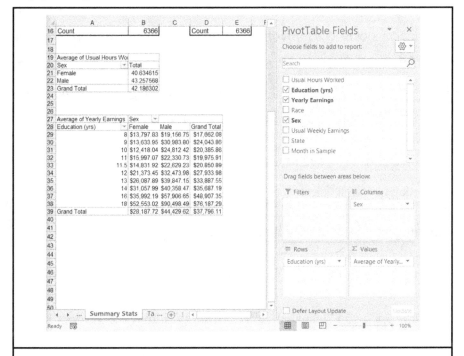

Target: Additional PivotTable for "Average of Yearly Earnings"

The values should always be added last since the table will always finalize the table, hiding the drag-and-drop prompts in the pivot table itself. You can always drag and drop fields in the add-in window to the left. We'll cover this in the next section.

Revamp Analyses by Dragging and Dropping Fields

In the EastNorthCentralFTWorkers workbook, the econometric students were asked to create a pivot table comparing the **Count, Count Num, Average and Sum** of the variable "Usual Weekly Earnings." These are default calculation functions built into PivotTable Field manager's "Value Field Settings." This table will help them compare the counts of data on the original dataset. This is the perfect opportunity to learn how to manipulate tables while learning how pivot tables work with real datasets.

The analysis calls for a pivottable with "Sex" in the rows with various calculations of "Usually Weekly Earnings" as the values. Since our first table already has Sex in its rows, we will modify this table for this analysis. To change the values, take the following steps:

1. Select the "Average of Usual Hours Worked" table

This will bring up the PivotTable fields for the table. We will be dragging and dropping the items we need from here.

2. In the PivotTable Fields window, uncheck "Usual Hours Worked"

3. Drag and drop "Usual Weekly Earnings" into the *Σ Values* section

4. Click the drop-down arrow, go to *Value field Settings >* *"Summarize values by" Tab* and select **Count**

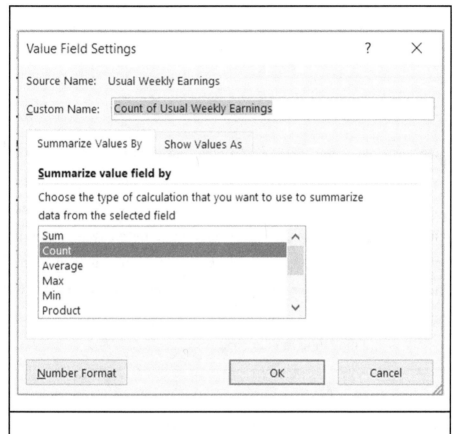

Target Value Field Settings for Count of Usual Weekly Earnings

The drag and dropped item might have automatically populated as **Count**. If it does not, you will have to change the settings yourself. Clicking on the drop-down menu and going to Value Field Settings, this is what the resulting dialogue box should look like.

5. Drag and drop another instance of "Usual Weekly Earnings" into the Σ *Values* section

6. Click the drop-down arrow, go to *Value field Settings > "Summarize values by" Tab* and select **Count Numbers**

Note:

On the Value Field Settings dialogue box, scrolling through, you should notice that there are various default calculations here. These are various statistical items that can be used to model data. Excel included these stats in the wizard as a guide for analysis. Going to the "Show Values As" tab you have the option to change the items to calculate various percentages of. This is good for showing rate of increase on bar graphs or for building pie charts. We will talk about analysis and modeling in later chapters.

---

7. Change the Custom Name field to "Count Num of Usual Weekly Earnings"

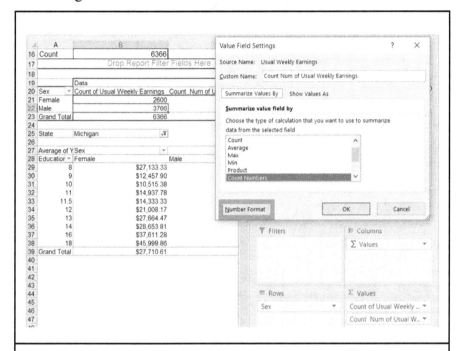

Target for Count Num of Usual Weekly Earnings and Naming Conventions

Looking at the pivottable at this point, the field names may seem verbose. It is best practice to have descriptive labels. This makes it easier for observers to comprehend the data. Further, it makes it easier to pass these labels on to your charts and graphs, automating the process. We'll discuss automation in later chapters. While you are at this dialogue box, be sure to change the number format to currency for the appropriate value sets. "Usual Weekly Earnings" are expected to be in dollars.

8. Repeat steps 5-7 to populate columns for **Average** and Sum

Target for PivotTable Fields for modified PivotTable 1

After populating Count, Count Num, Average, and Sum of Usual Weekly Earnings, the PivotTable Fields should look like the depiction above. You can toggle the PivotTable Fields window off and on by going to *PivotTable Analyze > Show > Field List*. While having the Pivot Table Fields window opened will help you revamp your pivot tables instantly, closing this window will also help you focus on the current arrangement of data.

9. Save your progress

The students were asked to calculate the various elements for Usual Weekly Earnings and compare them. For example, **Count** and **Count Num** should be the same since all the Weekly earnings should have been the same. However, looking at the data, not all individuals reported weekly earnings. For our purposes, this is important for how we structure and clean our data in preparation for pivot table analysis.

Recall that pivottables cannot operate with empty rows or columns. This modified dataset works around this limitation by using the conditional function $IF()$ to fill what would otherwise be 0 in the dataset. These "0" *weekly earnings* entries would mathematically skew the average. It also does not reflect what is happening realistically. These individuals, mathematically and logically, do not receive "0" *weekly earnings*. Replacing it with a string of text, in this case a simple ". "cleans the data of supperiferlous zeros and describes the scenario more accurately. This distinction can also let us hypothesize and compare individuals who report weekly earnings versus those who report only yearly earnings. We could postulate on questions such as, for example, "Do individuals who only report yearly earnings more or less than their peers?" We'll talk more about how we use data for analysis in a later chapter.

	Count of Usual Weekly Earnings	Count Num of Usual Weekly Earnings	Average of Usual Weekly Earnings	Sum of Usual Weekly Earnings
Female	2,600.00	612.00	$577.53	$353,451.00
Male	3,766.00	794.00	$849.81	$674,753.00
Grand Total	6,366.00	1,406.00	$731.30	$1,028,204.00

Target for Pivot Table showing Count, Count Num, Average and Sum for Usual Weekly Earnings broken down by Sex.

The image above depicts the final pivot table for the comparison exercise. You should notice that all of the values have been formatted appropriately. Proper number formatting helps with automation and creating models later on. In the meantime, how might you have the pivottable report on the percentage of individuals reporting weekly earnings in the dataset? Hint: You will need to drag-and drop another instance of "Usual Weekly Reportings" and use the *Value Field Settings > "Show Values As" tab* to calculate.

Excel for the Web: Share your PivotTables with Colleagues

The majority of the value of pivottables is being able to interact with large datasets in various ways. To interact with data you must be on an appropriate platform for data handling, particularly in our case due to the forwards incompatibility of Excel files. Recall our conversation about compatibility. Office 365 Excel 2019 files cannot run on older, perpetual licenses of Excel. This may cause conflict for colleagues or clients using older builds of Excel who want to explore the data. This can be circumvented by using Microsoft's Excel for the web client.

In order to use Excel for the web, you must have a Microsoft live account. If you have a subscription license, OneDrive and all of its sharing capabilities are included in the subscription suite. If you happen to have an Excel 2019 perpetual license, you must have a Microsoft live online account. Once you have an account, follow these steps to host your file onto your Onedrive account:

1. Click the *Share* button in the top left hand corner

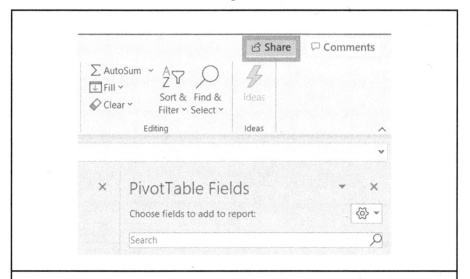

Share Button Location: Top Left Hand of the Excel Main Menu

This is the location of the Share button in Office 365 Excel 2019. This will take you to your OneDrive account. OneDrive is part of the Microsoft Office 365 suite that allows you to store and share your files in the cloud. You do not need a subscription service or even a perpetual license to obtain a OneDrive account. They offer a limited amount of cloud storage for free, enabling you to share and even embed your Microsoft files on the web.

2. If you haven't saved your file to OneDrive, Microsoft will prompt you to save here

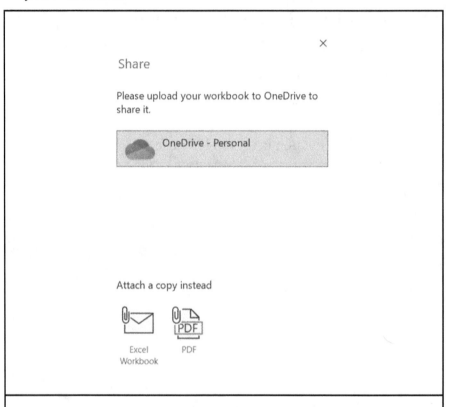

Save to One Drive Prompt Window

In addition to saving and sharing your file on the web, this prompt also gives you options to attach a copy of the file to an email through Outlook or another desktop email client. It is still advised to use Excel for the web, since the web viewer is uniform across operation systems and avoids compatibility issues. Also, pivottables are more valuable as interactive Excel for Web platforms than as static PDFs. Only use PDFs for presentations.

3. To access your file on Excel for the web click "Get a sharing link"

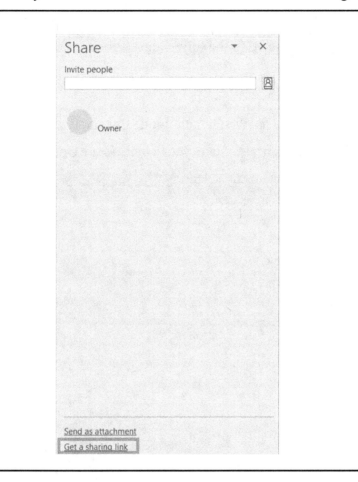

Share Sidebar: Accessing your file on OneDrive

After clicking the Share Button and saving your file to OneDrive, a share sidebar will appear on the left hand side. It will give you the option to attach and send the file. To access your file's OneDrive location, click on the "Get a sharing link" at the bottom of the sidebar.

There are two modes of Excel for the web: viewing, also listed as "Read Only" mode, and editing. Both come with their pros and cons, which we will discuss in the following sections.

Read Only Mode

Read only mode is the default mode for individuals who are not signed-in. You can also send your client Read Only Mode Excel for the Web environments by selecting:

"Get a Sharing Link" > "Create a view only link" button

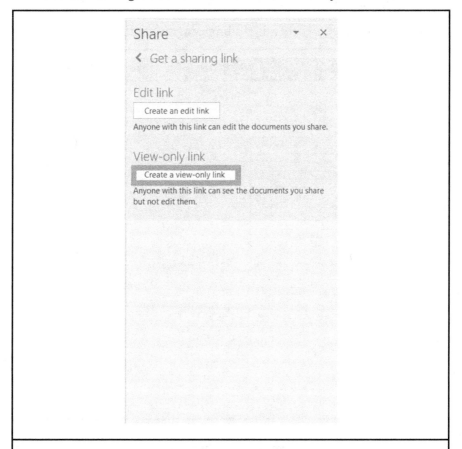

Share Sidebar: Get a Sharing Link, Read Only Mode

It is advised to use Read/View only mode links when possible. Microsoft uses Sharepoint as its backend powering OneDrive. As a result, it's not as flexible with various people making edits to a file from different locations. It can cause file conflicts that result in various instances of a file in the OneDrive. Thus, the workaround is to only share Read-Only files. You have the capability to manipulate pivot tables in Read-Only files.

Using Read-Only mode helps protect the original data of the sheet. Viewers can still manipulate pivot tables by clicking on the pivottable and using PivotTable Fields, including dragging and dropping fields.

Read-Only Mode Demonstration: Drag and Drop

Excel for web in Read-Only mode lets you drag and drop and manipulate PivotTable fields without disrupting the tables. This screenshot depicts a change in our first PivotTable, introducing "Months in Sample" as a filter variable for the pivottable. This view is ideal because clients can manipulative the data without destroying the pivottable structure. At any time, they can reset the pivottable view by refreshing the page.

The PivotTable Fields sidebar is available by toggling the "Field List" button to the left.

Another major benefit of Read-Only mode is that it's automatic for people who do not have a OneDrive account. No sign in is necessary to see this mode, even for people who accidently obtained an editing link. This is for perfect for live presentations where you may have to do simple demonstrations labs of data analysis. This is excellent for consultants who have to explain their work.

Editing Mode

You also have the option of sharing an editing file. This is good for teams who have an aggregate amount of data, especially for adding additional datasets to pivottable analysis. As aforementioned, having files in Editing Mode carries some risk. The sharepoint system can potentially add various files from various sources due to version mismanagement in the system. However, this does help with tracking file versions.

Note:

When sharing editing links, it is always advised to save a seperate file in case of editing mishaps, such as corruption due to a crash. While previous files can be restored from the cloud, it is better to err on the side of caution.

Office 356 Excel 2019 has some features that are not yet supported on Excel for Web. Therefore, after signing in, it will inform you that you must edit a copy of the workbook without the Office 365 Excel 2019 features.

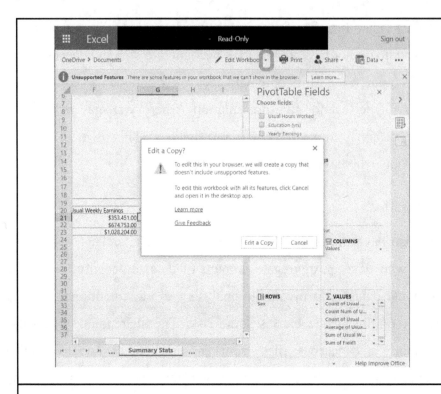

Accessing Editing Mode

Excel for web in Editing mode requires that you sign in to your Microsoft Account. After signing in, clicking the "Edit in Browser" drop-down menu brings you to this prompt, requesting that you edit a copy in Excel for web.

Going to *Edit in Browser drop − down > "Open in Desktop App"* gives you the option to open the file locally on your computer in your desktop build of Excel. However, this isn't a viable way to share your file to your clients or colleagues. Your clients and colleagues would need to have an Office 365 Excel 2019 build in order to open the file. This is also counter intuitive to sharing the file over a uniform platform.

Ultimately, in editing mode, you will have to deal with several versions of the same file. To keep down file management, it is better to only share Read-Only files. If you must use a file management scheme, we suggest labeling your files with the date that they were edited. For example, if today's date was 10-14-18 and you just saved an instance of our example file with your work, then the name of the file would be $EastNorthCentralFTWorkers\_[10-14-18].xlsx$.

Chapter 3

Automation and Efficiency

W hile automating repetitive tasks can take a lot of time, in the long run it saves time. Time is saved particularly because it reduces the chance of human error, simple mistakes that take a lot of time to find and resolve. Therefore, it is usually worth the time to set up a process that will be used over and over again. Ultimately, time saved is important for increasing productivity.

This chapter will cover Excel specific keyboard shortcuts for reducing computational time. These keyboard shortcuts help streamline your working sessions by reducing the time you spend looking for specific functions. These keyboard shortcuts can also be deployed in macro. This chapter will also cover some light coding scenarios.

Modern programming uses a concept called "modularization." To apply modular coding means that every function within the program is focused on addressing one concern. If you consider Excel, all functions in Excel use this concept. For example, $IFS()$ executes conditional statements given several qualifiers. $SUMIFS()$ combines $IFS()$ and $SUM()$, however, it simplifies conditional summing into one function for users.

Users can write programs and create custom functions that combine aspects of functions to do repetitive tasks. Deploying this concept for creating macros, you should create custom functions that achieve a specific goal and can be reused. The ability to create modular macros is a very valuable skill for Excel power users.

Note:

Same with compatibility, creating macros that deploy certain features will make it difficult to carry over your set up to older builds of Excel. In order to make macros that can be used across a system, be sure to use backwards compatible functions, i.e. functions that do not use Office 365 Excel 2019 specific functions.

Shortcuts and Tips

Learning and deploying keyboard shortcuts in your interactions with Excel will help with productivity and reduce work time. We have sorted the shortcuts into two categories: navigation, consolidation, and general shortcuts. We will display the shortcuts for PC and Mac when available.

Basic Pivot Table Shortcut Keys

Using pivot tables, you can extract information and create perspectives from massive datasets. Using these shortcut keys makes it easier to navigate between multiple tables and control data points. Following are the shortcut keys for Windows and Mac ("Keyboard shortcuts in Excel," n.d.).

Table: Basic PivotTable Shortcut Keys for Windows & Mac

This table lists shortcut keys for navigating pivottables. Some shortcuts may be recognizable to you, such as $[CTRL] + [A]$. However, this table will explain how they behave while interacting with pivottables. These shortcuts can be used in all versions of Excel.

Action	Windows	Mac
Select entire pivot table	$[CTRL] + [A]$	$[⌘] + [A]$
Toggle pivot table checkbox	$[Space - bar]$	$[Space - bar]$
Group pivot table items	$[ALT]$ $+[SHIFT]+...$ $[Right - Arrow]$	$[⌘] + [SHIFT]$ $+[K]$
Ungroup pivot table items	$[ALT]$ $+[SHIFT]+...$ $[Leftt - Arrow]$	$[⌘] + [SHIFT]$ $+[J]$
Add pivot chart to current workshop	$[F11]$	$[Fn] + [F11]$
Hide item from pivot table	$[CTRL] + [-]$	$[CTRL] + [-]$
Launch pivot table wizard	$[ALT] + [D] + [P]$	$[⌘] + [OPTION]$ $+[P]$

Accessing Multiple Consolidation Ranges

The Pivot Table wizard allows you to consolidate data from different sheets and different workbook files in one place. Specifically for Microsoft Excel for Mac, the consolidation ranges feature was removed. It can still be accessed using the keyboard shortcut ("Consolidate multiple data sources in a PivotTable," n.d.).

To explore this feature, we will have to create another data file. To do this, we will save a copy of *EastNorthCentralFTWorkers* as *EastNorthCentralFTWorkers_MC_Mod*. This will ensure that the data are in similar shapes and formats for the pivottable to analyze. Recall the data differentiator, "Usual Weekly Earnings". Some of the individuals do not report weekly data. This was determined from the "Original Variables" on the right side of the data sheet. These points were cleaned and organized according to the supplied code book. The "Recorded Variables" data on the right side is the interpreted census data, which was cleaned and modified to be used in pivottables.

We will be be modifying "Usual Weekly Earnings" by modifying the *IF*()function into an *IFS*()function. This is a simple way of adding an additional condition that should produce moderately more reported weekly earnings. It will also give you more practice with *IFS*(). This will make a mildly altered dataset that we can compare with the original.

To create a modified data file, take the following steps:

1. Go to *File > Save a Copy*

2. Name this new file *EastNorthCentralFTWorkers_MC_Mod*

3. In the new file, navigate to the "Data" sheet

4. Go to the "Usual Weekly Earnings" column, cell *F5*

5. Change the formula to: $= IFS(I5 > 0, I5, C5 < C6, (C5/50), I5 = 0, ".")$

SUM			✕ ✓ f_x		=IFS(I5>0,I5,C5<C6,(C5/50),I5=0,".")				

	A	B		IFS(logical_test1, value_if_true1, **[logical_test2**, value_if_true2], [logical_test3					
3				Recoded variables					
4	Usual Hours Worked	Education (yrs)	Yearly Earnings	Race	Sex	Usual Weekly Earnings	State	Month in Sample	A_GRSWK
5	40	13	$ 44,000	White	Male	=0,".")	Ohio	8	858
6	35	12	$ 12,000	White	Female	$ 240	Ohio	3	0

Modifying Data using conditional IFS()

This formula is intended to artificially change the number of individuals who report weekly income. This number will be random, since it is also based on the next value. The *IFS()*tests for three possibilities: (1) if the individual reported weekly income in the original dataset, (2) (if the person didn't report individual income) checks if the individual makes less than the following person in the dataset in yearly earnings, (3) (if the individual makes more than the next person) then they should report no earnings.

Condition (2) ensures that more people report weekly earnings at random. This randomizes this dataset and it will give us something to compare in the resulting pivot table.

6. After computing $F5$, copy-paste to the rest of the column to randomize the data.

7. Go to the **Summary Stats** sheet and click on one of the pivot tables

8. Update the tables to reflect this change by going to:

   PivotTable Analyze > Data > Refresh drop − down > Refresh All

9. Save your progress and note the location of the modified file.

Now we can use **Multiple Consolidation Ranges** to compare these two files.

1. Go back to the original file and go to the **Summary Stats** sheet

2. Open the PivotTable Wizard press:

   For Windows:$[ALT] + [D], [P]$

   For Mac: $[\mathcal{H}] + [\neg] + [P]$

3. Click Multiple consolidation ranges and then Next

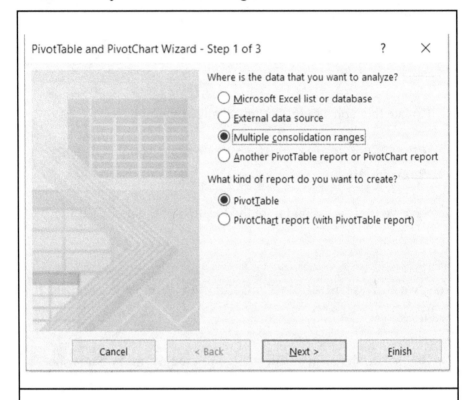

Old PivotTable and PivotChart Wizard

Using the keyboard shortcuts, this is the fastest and least resource intensive way to consolidate several files.

4. Choose "Create a single page field for me"

5. Click the up-arrow icon next to the "Range:" box to select the Recorded Data section

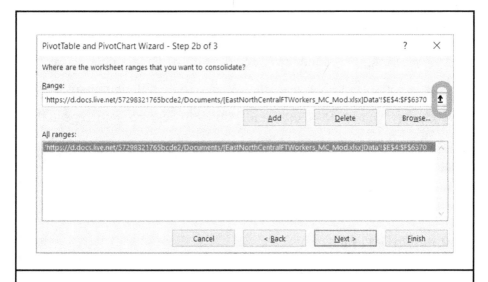

Target: Consolidate Ranges from the modified Workbook

Once you select the file, you must also select the ranges you want to combine. The input for the range will depend on the location of your file. To get the proper location, it is better to keep $EastNorthCentralFTWorkers\_MC\_Mod.xlsx$ opened and search it using the up-arrow button. Variably, the input range will look like:

$$\ldots -Location-\ldots[EastNorthCentralFTWorkers\_MC\_Mod.xlsx]Data$$

The "fields" are cells used to label the data. In our case, we have 6 total fields. The wizard can only handle 6. You will have to specifically select the ranges from the sheet. In our case, those ranges will be: $\ldots Data'!\$E\$4:\$F\$6370$. Selecting more than that will cause Excel to crash.

6. Click **Add** and hit **Next**

7. Select a location for the new table

Note: Pivottables cannot overlap. Be sure to have ample space for your pivottable. Otherwise, the Wizard will tell you there is no room for your table, close, and you will be forced to repeat the process all over again.

You may have to move around pivot tables by selecting them and going to: *PivotTable Analyze > Actions drop − down menu > Move PivotTable*

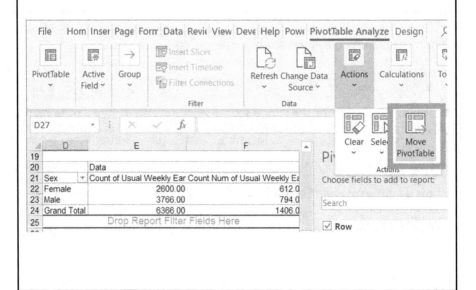

8. Click **Finish**

> **Note:**
>
> If you want to edit the source of a consolidated pivot table, you must use the shortcut keys to open the pivottable wizard again.
>
> For Windows: $[ALT] + [D], [P]$
>
> For Mac: $[\mathbb{H}] + [\neg] + [P]$

Power Pivot Navigational Shortcuts

Navigation shortcuts reduce the time spent on searching for different buttons and tasks. You must learn these shortcuts to incorporate these shortcuts into your computations. Typically, if they save you time, you will naturally use them, like the traditional $[CTRL] + [C], [CTRL] + [V]$ for copy-paste in Windows.

Here is a table of keyboard shortcuts and their function in Power Pivot ("Power Pivot keyboard shortcuts and accessibility—Office Support," n.d.).

Note:

Power Pivot is only available in Windows desktop builds. Therefore, this table is only for Windows keyboard shortcuts.

Table: Power Pivot Navigation Keyboard Shortcuts

This table lists keyboard shortcuts and how they behave in the Power Pivot widget. This table has been categorized for your convenience. The "Basic Computation & Navigation" category, for example, includes many shortcuts which you may already recognize, but explicitly lists how they behave in Power Pivot. The other categories include table navigation shortcuts followed by lesser known computation shortcuts.

Category: Basic Navigation & Computation	
Key Combination	Description
$[Mouse: Right - Click]$	After selecting an item, **open the context menu** for the selected item (cell, column, or row).
$[CTRL] + [A]$	Select the entire table (**all** for entire).
$[CTRL] + [C]$	**Copy** selected data
$[CTRL] + [D]$	**Delete** the table.
$[CTRL] + [M]$	**Move** the table.
$[CTRL] + [R]$	**Rename** the table.
$[CTRL] + [S]$	**Save** the table.

$[CTRL] + [Y]$	**Redo** the last action.
$[CTRL] + [Z]$	**Undo** the last action.
$[CTRL] + [Space - bar]$	Select the current **column**.
$[SHIFT] + [Space - bar]$	Select the current **row**.
Category: Table Navigation	
Key Combination	Description
$[SHIFT] + [Pg\ Up]$	Selects all cells from the current location to the **first cell** of the column.
$[SHIFT] + [Pg\ Dn]$	Selects all cells from the current location to the **last cell** of the column.
$[SHIFT] + [END]$	Select all cells from the current location to the **last cell** of the row.
$[SHIFT] + [HOME]$	Select all cells from the current location to the **first cell** of the row.
$[CTRL] + [Pg\ Up]$	**Move** to the previous table
$[CTRL] + [Pg\ Dn]$	**Move** to the next table
$[CTRL] + [HOME]$	Move to the first cell in the **upper left corner** of the selected table

[*CTRL*] + [*END*]	Move to the last cell in the **lower right corner** of the selected table (or the last row of the 'Add Column')
[*CTRL*] + [*Left* − *Arrow*]	**Move** to the first cell of the selected row.
[*CTRL*] + [*Right* − *Arrow*]	**Move** to the last cell of the selected row.
[*CTRL*] + [*Up* − *Arrow*]	**Move** to the first cell of the selected column.
[*CTRL*] + [*Down* − *Arrow*]	**Move** to the last cell of the selected column.

Category: Other Computation Shortcuts

Key Combination	Description
[*CTRL*] + [*ESC*]	**Close or cancel.** Can be for closing a dialog box or canceling a process such as a paste operation.
[*F5*]	Open **Go To** Dialog Box
[*F9*]	**Recalculate** all formulas in the Power Pivot window.

Automate PivotTables with Macros in VBA

Power users of Excel know how to use macros to handle repetitive tasks. Macros are small, custom programs that you can execute in Excel. The programs are written in VBA (Visual Basic for Applications).

> **Note:**
>
> In many online resources macros and VBA are used interchangeably. Macros are the executable script of instructions. VBA is the platform used to write a macro.

In order to use a macro, you must:

1. Enable the developer ribbon in Excel

2. Save the workbook as a "macro enabled file"

The workbook file must be macro-enabled to implement them. Microsoft established this "macro-enabled" file type for all of their products, including Excel, in order to prevent malicious macros from hijacking computer systems though VBA. This is why many offices outright ban macro enabled files. At the bare minimum, Microsoft will always prompt you when you are about to open any macro enabled file.

The best policy for creating automated Excel sheets is to have a single, "production PC", a desktop that is able to run macros. The resulting data and tables should be saved to a regular Excel workbook. When creating macros, keep this format in mind.

The VBA console, called Visual Basic Editor (VBE) by the Microsoft Support website, can be accessed using [*ALT*] + [*F*11] in PC . To access the VBE console in Mac, the keyboard shortcut is [*Option*] + [*F*11]]. However, the "Developer Ribbon" must be enabled to run and set up shortcuts for running your macros.

Accessing the Developer Ribbon in Windows and Mac

The ribbon must be enabled on the main tabs menu. In order to achieve this in Windows do the following steps:

1. Go to *File > Options > Customize Ribbon*

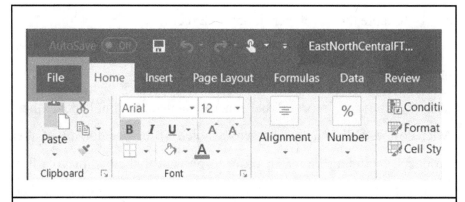

Excel Main Menu

Note:

Most actions start here. Remember that you can only access this menu when you have an active file opened.

2. Check the "Developer's" box on the right and click **OK**

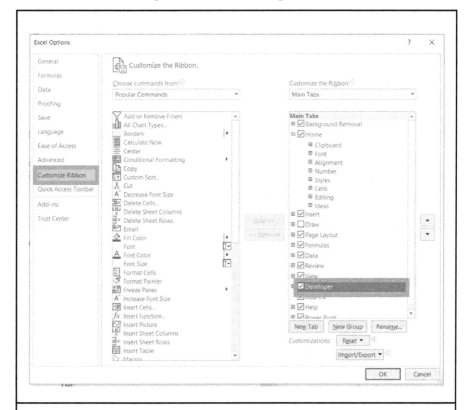

Target for Excel Options: Customize Ribbon >Main Tabs

This screenshot depicts the target window for the Customize Ribbons section. By default, Developer is disabled. However, it is considered part of the Main Tabs in Microsoft.

The Developer ribbon should appear. This ribbon gives you a variety of tools for managing your Excel sheet, including Active X controls. However, your file must be macro-enabled to use these tools due to the security concerns discussed prior.

Developer Ribbon

This screenshot depicts the resulting Developer ribbon. There are several advanced tools used to automate your Microsoft outfit across several of their platforms. We will be focusing only on building and managing macros.

The steps are similar in Mac OS Excel 2019 builds. You can access the VBA compiler on a Mac through:

$Opt + F11$ or $Fn + Opt + F11$

The macro manager can be accessed on Mac using:

$$OPTION + F8$$

Starting with Macros: Learning VBA Syntax

This text focuses on pivottables; therefore, we will be discussing common pivottable oriented macros. To begin using VBA you must first learn this language syntax. Consider the following Pivot Table code pulled from a macro demonstration resource ("The VBA Guide To Excel Pivot Tables," n.d.).

```
1    Sub CreatePivotTable()
2    'PURPOSE: Creates a brand new Pivot table on a new worksheet from data in the ActiveSheet
3    'Source: www.TheSpreadsheetGuru.com
4
5    Dim sht As Worksheet
6    Dim pvtCache As PivotCache
7    Dim pvt As PivotTable
8    Dim StartPvt As String
9    Dim SrcData As String
10
11   'Determine the data range you want to pivot
12      SrcData = ActiveSheet.Name & "!" & Range("A1:R100").Address(ReferenceStyle:=xlR1C1)
13
14   'Create a new worksheet
15      Set sht = Sheets.Add
16
17   'Where do you want Pivot Table to start?
18      StartPvt = sht.Name & "!" & sht.Range("A3").Address(ReferenceStyle:=xlR1C1)
19
20   'Create Pivot Cache from Source Data
21      Set pvtCache = ActiveWorkbook.PivotCaches.Create( _
22         SourceType:=xlDatabase, _
23         SourceData:=SrcData)
24
25   'Create Pivot table from Pivot Cache
26      Set pvt = pvtCache.CreatePivotTable( _
27         TableDestination:=StartPvt, _
28         TableName:="PivotTable1")
29
30   End Sub
```

Code Snippet: Create a Pivot Table

Screenshot of the code in VBA. In many cases you will be modifying code pulled from Excel help sites. To use these effectively, you should learn how to read them.

1. *Sub CreatePivotTable()*

This is the calling function for the macro. This is important when deploying macro in other macro. All functions take the form of "name"(arguments), if the function takes any arguments. This should be familiar because this is how we call formula functions in Excel.

2. *'PURPOSE: Creates a brand new Pivot table on a new worksheet from data...*

3. *'Source: www.TheSpreadsheetGuru.com*

These are comments. Comments are indicated with a backtick `and are not compiled with the rest of the code. They are used to include notes in the code to make reading the code comprehensible. The programmer of the macro was thorough enough to explain each action using comments.

Dim sht As Worksheet

Dim pvtCache As PivotCache

...

Dim SrcData As String

This is where the variables of the program are declared. These variables are used to carry out the operations of the program. This section is useful in identifying what parts of the program to edit because it also tells you the type of variable. Thus, if you wanted to change some aspect of the program, you would begin here.

After the declaration of variables is the main body of the program, this is where all of the instructions are listed. This programmer explained each section of code and what it does. Some instructions you would want to change are **line 12** and **line 18**, as they determine the range used to create a pivot table and where the resulting pivot table will populate. In this case, this macro operates only on the active worksheet in the window.

Common VBA Automated Pivot Table Actions: Create a Pivot Table

Let's modify our example code for our purposes. Deploying this macro will create a new pivottable in one click from a named range.

1. Save a copy of the workbook as macro enabled workbook with the name:

EastNorthCentralFTWorkers_Macro.xlsm

Note:

Actions executed by macros are not saved in the undo-redo cache. This means that any action a macro executes cannot be undone. Further, macro-enabled files cannot be autosaved. This makes it difficult to obtain recent past versions of the file. *If you are testing and developing macros, it is best practice to always save a separate macro-enabled file.*

---

2. Use the shortcut to access the Macro dialogue box

Macro Dialogue Box

Screenshot of the Macro dialogue box. This dialogue box is used to manage, run, and create macro. Once this box is populated with macro you can assign custom shortcut keys to each macro by going to the **Options** button.

3. Type in *CreatePivotTable* into the macro box and click **Create**. This will start an instance of VBA in a new window

4. Copy the following into VBA:

```
Sub CreatePivotTable()

Dim sht As Worksheet

Dim pvtCache As PivotCache

Dim pvt As PivotTable

Dim StartPvt As String

Dim SrcData As String


'Determine the data range you want to pivot

'This part of the code was changed for our pivottable

 SrcData = ActiveSheet.Name & "!" &
Range("A4:H6370").Address(ReferenceStyle:=Pivot_Table_Values)




'Create a new worksheet
```

```vb
    Set sht = Sheets.Add


'Where do you want Pivot Table to start?

    StartPvt = sht.Name & "!" &
sht.Range("A3").Address(ReferenceStyle:=xlR1C1)


'Create Pivot Cache from Source Data

    Set pvtCache = ActiveWorkbook.PivotCaches.Create( _

        SourceType:=xlDatabase, _

        SourceData:=SrcData)


'Create Pivot table from Pivot Cache

    Set pvt = pvtCache.CreatePivotTable( _

        TableDestination:=StartPvt, _

        TableName:="PivotTableTest")
End Sub
```

5. Click save and to execute your macro, click the small green triangle to run

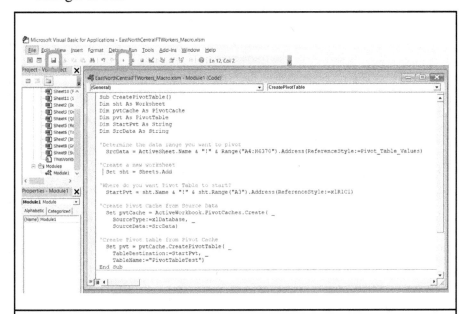

Microsoft VBA Editor

This is a screenshot of the VBA editor. This allows you to create, edit, and execute macro. In this code, you must be on the **Data** sheet in order to execute. Otherwise, the macro will give you an error. As this is programming, all instructions must be very verbose. Any errors in syntax or addressing will generate a "Debugging" prompt. To see this prompt, try changing one of the variables in the declaration portion of the code and running the macro.

6. After the Macro executes, it will create a new sheet and a new pivot table that you can populate manually.

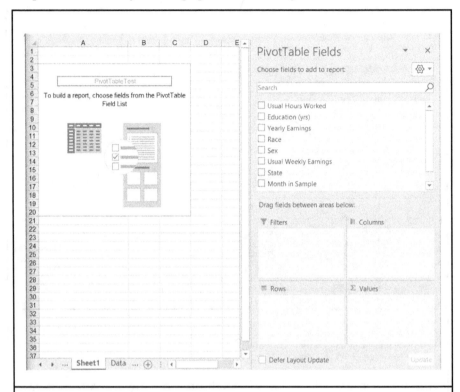

Target: Macro Generated PivotTable

This is a screenshot of the new sheet generated by *Sub CreatePivotTable*(). This macro allows us to automatically create pivottable with a keyboard shortcut instead of manually selecting items each time. This is particularly useful for repetitive reports that use the same, named ranges every time.

Following are some similar pivottable automation codes that automate with pivottable management. Create these macros on this file and explore them yourself ("The VBA Guide To Excel Pivot Tables," n.d.):

Delete a Specific Pivot Table

```vba
Sub DeletePivotTable()

'PURPOSE: How to delete a specific Pivot Table

'SOURCE: www.TheSpreadsheetGuru.com


'Delete Pivot Table By Name

  ActiveSheet.PivotTables("PivotTable1").TableRange2.Clear


End Sub
```

Note:

The *DeletePivotTable*() macro requires that you have your pivottables named. You can name your pivot tables by selecting them and going to:

$$PivotTable\ Analyze > PivotTable\ drop - down$$
$$> "PivotTable\ Name"$$

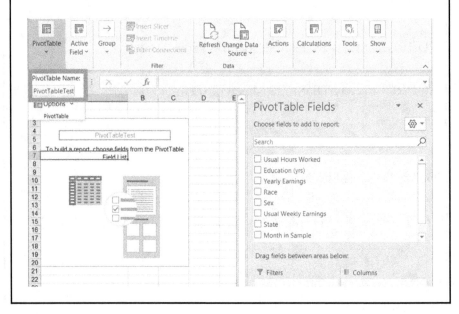

Delete All Pivot Tables

```vba
Sub DeleteAllPivotTables()

'PURPOSE: Delete all Pivot Tables in your Workbook

'SOURCE: www.TheSpreadsheetGuru.com


Dim sht As Worksheet

Dim pvt As PivotTable


'Loop Through Each Pivot Table In Currently Viewed Workbook

  For Each sht In ActiveWorkbook.Worksheets

    For Each pvt In sht.PivotTables

      pvt.TableRange2.Clear

    Next pvt

  Next sht


End Sub
```

This code is useful for cleaning up workbooks after your analysis. However, it is ill advised to assign *Sub DeleteAllPivotTables()* and similar macros like it to keyboard shortcut. Actions by macro cannot be undone and this macro can potentially destroy your work.

Common VBA Automated Pivot Table Actions: Modifying Fields

Before creating macros that automate fields you must have an understanding of what fields are. Pivottable fields are populated when you create a pivottable from a range. Excel recognizes fields to manipulate them, usually the top row of a column that describes the data below as in our example. Recall from the multiple ranges consolidation that the old pivot table wizard only recognizes up to 4 fields.

Conversely, you can program macros to manage fields if the data is going to have the same structure. Recall from earlier in the chapter our conversation about modularization. Having a modular macro means that each task is handled by only one macro. Calling these macro in a full script, a list macro executed together, you can potentially create a pivottable with a few keyboard shortcuts in a few seconds.

Logically in your script, after executing*CreatePivotTable()*, you can manage the fields with macros and generate a report in seconds.

Let's look at *Adding_PivotFields()*.
Similar to the *CreatePivotTable()*macro, this macro must be edited for the context of your dataset. Let's look at a numbered version of the code to analyze it.

```
 1    Sub Adding_PivotFields()
 2    'PURPOSE: Show how to add various Pivot Fields to Pivot Table
 3    'SOURCE: www.TheSpreadsheetGuru.com
 4
 5    Dim pvt As PivotTable
 6
 7    Set pvt = ActiveSheet.PivotTables("PivotTable1")
 8
 9      'Add item to the Report Filter
10      pvt.PivotFields("Year").Orientation = xlPageField
11
12      'Add item to the Column Labels
13      pvt.PivotFields("Month").Orientation = xlColumnField
14
15      'Add item to the Row Labels
16      pvt.PivotFields("Account").Orientation = xlRowField
17
18      'Position Item in list
19      pvt.PivotFields("Year").Position = 1
20
21      'Format Pivot Field
22      pvt.PivotFields("Year").NumberFormat = "#,##0"
23
24      'Turn on Automatic updates/calculations --like screenupdating to speed up code
25      pvt.ManualUpdate = False
26
27    End Sub
```

Annotated VBA Language: Adding_PivotFields()

This is a screenshot of *Adding_PivotFields()*. You may have noticed that this screenshot does not look the same as the VBA editor. This shot was taken using Notepad ++, a free text program for editing code. Notepad++ annotates the text in any language of your choice and also provides line numbers, where the current VBA does not. As VBA is not always available due to security concerns, Notepad++ is an excellent text editor for editing and studying code when you do not have access to VBA. However, you need VBA to compile and debug the code.

Adding_PivotFields()sorts predefined fields into a predefined pivot table named*pivotable*1. Let's return to our first simple pivot table example. It called for "Sex" in the rows and the average of "Usual Hours Worked". We are targeting our new pivottable in the newly created sheet, so we will have to change the predefined pivottable name to *PivotTableTest* . Thus, our new code for *Adding_PivotFields*()would be:

[Modified] Add Pivot Fields

```
Sub Adding_PivotFields()
'PURPOSE: Show how to add various Pivot Fields to Pivot Table
'SOURCE: www.TheSpreadsheetGuru.com


Dim pvt As PivotTable


Set pvt = ActiveSheet.PivotTables("PivotTableTest")


'Add item to the Report Filter
    'pvt.PivotFields("Year").Orientation = xlPageField--Unnecessary


  'Add item to the Column Labels
    'pvt.PivotFields("Month").Orientation = xlColumnField--
```

Unnecessary


```
 'Add item to the Row Labels

   pvt.PivotFields("Sex").Orientation = xlRowField
'Position Item in list

   'pvt.PivotFields("Year").Position = 1 --Unnecessary



 'Add Values Item in list

   pvt.AddDataField pvt.PivotFields("Usual Hours Worked"),
"Average of Usual Hours Worked", xlAverage


 'Format Pivot Field

   ' pvt.PivotFields("Year").NumberFormat = "#,##0" --Unnecessary


 'Turn on Automatic updates/calculations --like screenupdating to
speed up code

   pvt.ManualUpdate = False


End Sub
```

Note:

In this modified code we kept the old lines and commented them out. This is good for keeping track of changes in your macros. However, this can lead to a lot of junk code in your macros. Once you are done developing your macros, clean up your comments. Make sure the comments are clear and describe each part of the code.

To execute this code, return to the newly generated sheet with the pivottable entitled *PivotTableTest*. Go to: *Developer > Macros > Macro Name*: *Adding_PivotFields* and click the **Run** button. This will populate the empty *PivotTableTest* table.

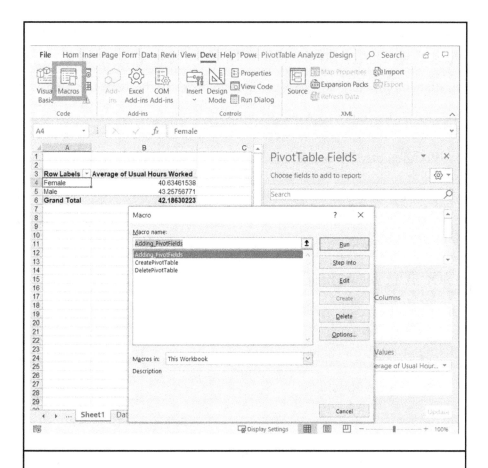

Editing the "PivotTestTable" PivotTable with Macros

This is a screenshot of the resulting pivottable after populating it with *Adding_PivotFields*(). After establishing the code, it only took seconds for Excel to generate this data with a new pivottable. The best way to deploy these macros in a modular way is to create a script that deploys *CreatePivotTable*() first and *Adding_PivotFields*() second.

This code combines some of the other operators and arguments at the SpreadsheetGuru's list of common macro codes. Following are some similar pivottable field management macros. Study them on your own and use them to modify your pivottables:

Add Calculated Pivot Fields

```
Sub AddCalculatedField()
'PURPOSE: Add a calculated field to a pivot table
'SOURCE: www.TheSpreadsheetGuru.com


Dim pvt As PivotTable
Dim pf As PivotField


'Set Variable to Desired Pivot Table
  Set pvt = ActiveSheet.PivotTables("PivotTable1")


'Set Variable Equal to Desired Calculated Pivot Field
  For Each pf In pvt.PivotFields
    If pf.SourceName = "Inflation" Then Exit For
  Next
```

```vba
'Add Calculated Field to Pivot Table

  pvt.AddDataField pf


End Sub
```

Add A Values Field

```vba
Sub AddValuesField()

'PURPOSE: Add A Values Field to a Pivot Table

'SOURCE: www.TheSpreadsheetGuru.com


Dim pvt As PivotTable

Dim pf As String

Dim pf_Name As String


pf = "Salaries"

pf_Name = "Sum of Salaries"
```

```
Set pvt = ActiveSheet.PivotTables("PivotTable1")


pvt.AddDataField pvt.PivotFields("Salaries"), pf_Name, xlSum


End Sub
```

This example *AddValuesField*()macro code deploys xl consolidation functions to instruct the *Σ Values* section on what calculation to perform. In the plainest of terms, these are VBA arguments that allow you to automate different calculations in the Value field. They are fairly comprensible and the most common ones you will use are ("XlConsolidationFunction enumeration (Excel) | Microsoft Docs," n.d.):

xlAverage: Finds the average

xlCount: Finds the number of entries

xlCountNums: Find the number of entries that are numerical

xlSum: Sum, which is the default calculation when setting a Values with VBA

You can find a whole list of other arguments at the Microsoft VBA support site.

Chapter 4

Analysis

Analysis is the process of evaluating data and creating new perspective of that data. Those who get the most out of data analysis are those who understand the investigative process. Unfortunately, many people tend to mistake Excel and pivot tables to be the primary tool for creating these new perspectives. These tools may allow you to create a presentation. The impact of that presentation, however, depends on your grasp of the analysis and the way you present your content. This distinction separates data entry freelancers from business analyst consultants who inform business decisions.

One natural approach to analysis is asking the right questions. In this chapter, we will discuss the process of analysis and overview some features that will assist in presenting your analysis. Recall our discussion of functionality. Pivottables, and Power Pivot wizards, are features that allow you to achieve a specific goal: creating new perspectives of large swaths of what would otherwise be unintelligible spreadsheet tables of information.

After completing this chapter, you will be able to:

- Gather and arranging data for evaluation

- Reason context for investigation and evaluation

- Create new perspectives on the data

Finally, we will briefly overview data mining: using tech to pull trends from large data sets.

Overview: Process of Analysis

Pivottables allow you to view data in different ways, which enables you to analyze and report on large amounts of data in a meaningful way. Analysis, therefore, is broken down into 3 steps:

1. **Providing Context**: Gathering and arranging data in a meaningful way

2. **Evaluating**: Asking questions about the data

3. **Creating**: Discovering and validating new perspectives on the data

Excel allows an analysis of large data sets through aggregating them with pivot tables and slicers. Pivot tables are a tool that allows you to gather and assemble data from large data sets. Recall the section on accessing multiple consolidation ranges. By using the keyboard shortcuts ()in Windows, (in Mac: [⌘] + [⌥] + [P]), you can open the Pivot Table Wizard. This allows you direct access to the consolidation ranges feature.

Meanwhile, slicers allow you to instantly change and filter multiple pivot tables. Slicers are also available through the Pivot Table wizard once you have multiple pivot tables. While this feature allows you to control multiple pivot tables, the slicer's *functionality* are the different perspectives it creates to achieve better visibility into data.

Note:

Slicers are only available on the desktop version. Therefore, they can only be viewed in Excel for the web.

Providing Context: Creating and Managing Multiple Pivot Tables

Slicers allow you to filter table and pivot table data. Most importantly, slicers clearly label filtered states, making the tables more presentable in reports. To use slicers for pivottables the following conditions must be met ("Use slicers to filter data—Office Support," n.d.):

1. You need to be on a desktop build of Excel

2. PivotTables need to be enabled

3. The data must be in a PivotTable

4. Must not be in compatible mode

Note:

In order to save our example file, Excel put the file into compatibility mode. This is done for files that may be viewed on different machines. To get your file out of compatibility mode you must go to *File > Info > Compatibility Mode*

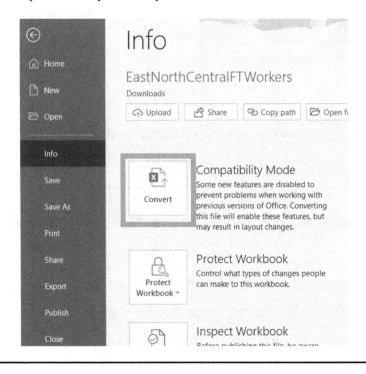

After all these conditions are met, the best way to see the value of slicers is to have multiple PivotTables. Let's return to our large dataset example. The Q&A asks for 3 different pivot tables. Let's rearrange our Summary Stats page into a report by state.

1. Rearrange the tables using *PivotTable Analyze > Action > Move Table...*for each item

---

Note:

This is also a good time to name each table. The suggested names are:

Avg_Y_Earnings

Avg_Hours_Worked

Avg_Hours_Worked

Keep track of these names. This is how the slicer will control the pivottables

---

2. Select a pivot table

3. Go to *Insert > "Filters" > Slicer*

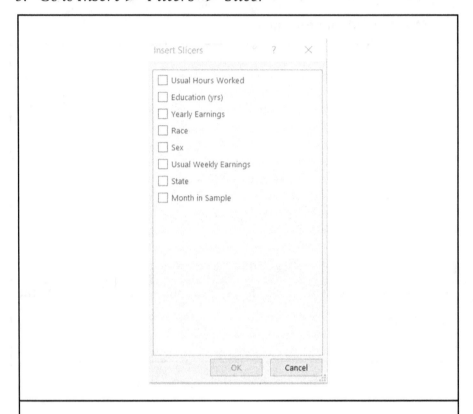

Slicer Dialogue Box

This is a screenshot of the slicer dialogue box. The slicers automatically connect to the dataset through the pivottable. Since these are essentially filters, it is better to choose fields that are independent variables: location, race, sex, and education. In this case, we are choosing location, "State".

4. Click on **State**

5. Select the slicer to make the Slicer Ribbon appear and navigate to *Slicer > Report Connections*

6. Select all PivotTables

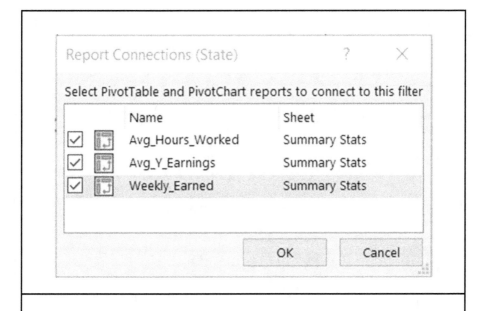

Report Connections Dialogue Box

This is a screenshot of the controls for the State slicer.

Note:

All pivot tables have a filter section. However, this filter section is limited to the individual pivottable. Using slicers allow you to deploy multiple pivot tables in interactive reports.

7. Save your progress

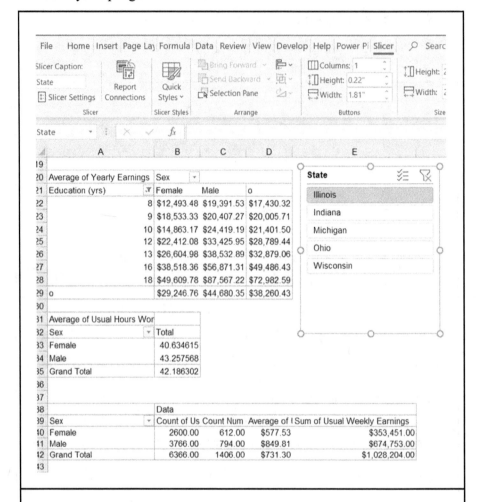

Target: State Slicer

This is a screenshot of the resulting slicer after selecting state. The Slicer ribbon also appears, where you can manage what pivottables your slicer controls.

Creating: Discovering and Validating New Perspectives on the Data

Similar to filters with regular Excel spreadsheets, slicers allow you to slice data into various views instantly. Manipulating the data helps with finding new perspectives.

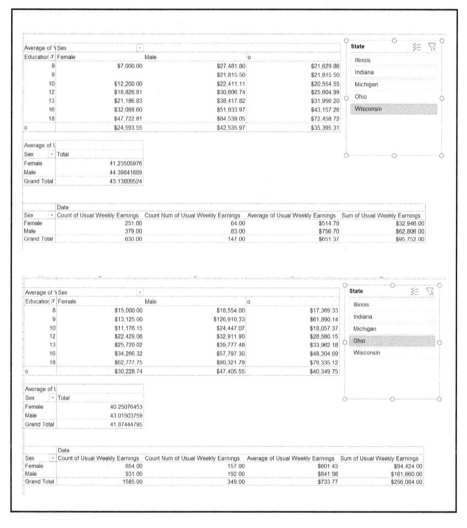

Comparison of Wisconsin and Ohio Reports

Looking at the State data side by side, you can see that there is a gap for Females with 9 years of education in Wisconsin. Recall our misleading scatter plot example. How might you represent this gap in the data? Further, consider the quality of the data. Is this gap due to less rigorous sample size? What portion of the report would support this assertion?

Analysis can be used to model results in a way that is both visually attractive and effective. Recall our conversation about analysis and creating new perspectives. These perspectives are more easily discovered when visualized.

Chapter 5

Investigative Modeling using Pivot Charts

If you were paying attention, you would notice that we only discussed two aspects of analysis in chapter 4, providing context and creation. However, in the overview of analysis, we stated that there were 3 steps in the process:

1. **Providing Context**: Gathering and arranging data in a meaningful way

2. **Evaluating**: Asking questions about the data

3. **Creating**: Discovering and validating new perspectives on the data

Evaluation of data depends solely on the type of data you are analyzing and, therefore, deserves its own chapter. Aspects of evaluation and investigation for all sorts of datasets are found in data modeling. Modeling data is an important step for creating new perspectives on data. It allows you to visibly see the data in a meaningful way and investigate through a series of informed questions. The majority of these questions are "how" and "why" questions, since the others (what, when, who) can already be answered by the charts of data in front of you.

After you've investigated and found your conclusions, modeling is also critical for communicating these perspectives on data. For the audiences that you are presenting your information to, modeling is often the only way to communicate your findings. More information can be gleaned from a visualization like a chart or a graph than from numbers from a table.

The communicative property of visualization is particularly the case for large data sets. For big data, which can be several thousand rows and columns, data can only be presented with a map. This chapter will cover basic principles in data modeling, creating visualizations, and building maps.

Principals in Data Modeling

When using modeling to investigate data, a chart or a graph is more adept at answering "how" and "why" questions. For example, consider our large data set. This dataset can technically answer all the other non-analysis questions on its own with the help of a few filters and a formula. For example:

"Who"

Do men who have greater than 12 years of education make more than [Y] dollars?

"Where"

Where are women least likely to make less than [Y] dollars?

"When"

Given the month in sample, when do the highest ranges occur?

"What"

What is the lowest earning in each state?

However, if we were to generate a few linear regressions over an (X,Y) plane, then we could answer questions such as:

"How do years of education [X] determine yearly salary [Y] for females"?

If in our theoretical graph the line goes [up], it would indicate that [Y] had an increase over the years of [X]. This is the value that modeling brings to analysis: it provides trends that tell us "how" things happen and may even glean "why" things happen with a little more context. Ergo, charts tracking several items are more prepared to answer "why" since we can compare the axises to each other and comment on causality. However, you must be careful with this line of questioning in statistics. More context is usually needed to confirm acertations of "why," usually confirming with contextual research such as interviews. Acertainations gleaned from statistical analysis are still useful because they can inform a beginning hypothesis for you to test. Even more importantly, there are rules in modeling to ensure that presented data can give you the most accurate acertaintions to test.

Charts that are incorrectly modeled can skew data and, therefore, can skew insights. This can be disastrous for analysts, since they can easily come to the wrong conclusions. When we move on to presenting our data, being a data analyst requires a level of integrity: charts can visually skew data for audiences as well. Analysts who use this knowledge to purposefully skew charts to confirm their worldview lack scientific integrity. Knowing these modeling rules can help you recognize human error as well as purposeful meddling. Following these rules ensures accurate modeling:

1. **Use an expected range on the independent axis.** The independent axis is the "X" axis on charts. This axis usually represents units of time or some other independent variable. Always start the graph at 0 or at "time-zero" as the marked beginning of your dataset. The x-axis should always be increasing. Do not "break" the independent axis, i.e. you must have a continuous number line starting from zero. If you have a large gap in the [Y] axis from your starting point, instead, use a rate that accurately reflects the data. Excel's charts and graphs do this automatically for you.

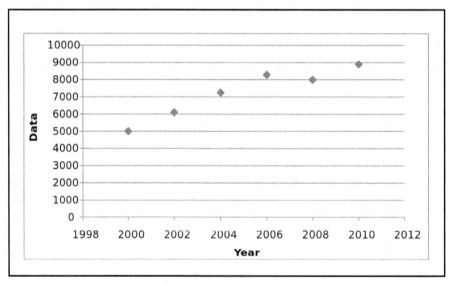

Scatterplot with a broken Independent axis: Missing Values

This is an example of a graph with a broken X axis. More specifically, this dataset is a scatter plot with all of the odd years removed ("File:Scatter Plot with missing categories.svg—Wikimedia Commons," n.d.). As a scatter plot, all data points on the graph must be represented by a point. If the value for 1999 was zero, for example, it must be included. Removing the odd "Years," not only breaks the X axis, it removes 50% of the data, which makes this graph broken.

2. **Use an expected range on the dependent axis.** Dependent axis is usually the item you're measuring or topic of the graph. Don't 'break' the dependent axis. Use a rate that accurately reflects the data.

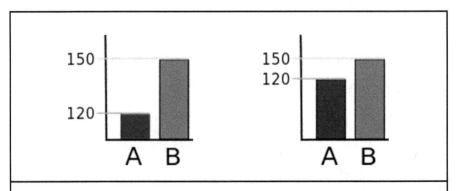

Bar Graph with no defined range

This is a side by side comparison of a graph representing undefined Y axis. Technically both A and B are the same same values. However, there is no point representing zero and there is no established rate of increase ("Bar graph missing zero1—Misleading graph—Wikipedia," n.d.; "File:Example truncated bar graph.svg—Wikimedia Commons," n.d.).

3. **Clearly label units**: percentages, currency, time, etc

4. Percentages should always add up to 100% on a pie chart

   a. Exception: Rate of increase, e.g. some item increased [Y%] over [X] time

   b. Rate of increase will always be over time, and therefore, will be represented on a graph, not a pie chart.

c. Be sure to label clearly the period of time for each increase

d. The rate of time will be uniform, i.e., 1 year

5. **Always use a descriptive title**: .e.g. "Measurement of [Y] over [X] for [Length of X]"

Visualization rules always depend on what sort of data you're representing. Recall the listed rule about percentages. Percentages are a ratio, a method of showing relation between data points without getting hung up on the value of numbers. A value of 100 is greater than 7, for example, but with percentages we know that 100 is 93% greater than 7. This example is easy because 100 is a 'clean' number that is easier to comprehend, like all the powers of 10. However, when you change the values to numbers you are more likely to see in the wild, $171.64 increasing to $2,452.00, the 93% increase is easier to graph.

Taking this example, how to represent this data is dependent on the context. This 93% increase is easier shown on a graph if it occured over time. Conversely, if the data is accompanied by other values that are part of a whole, it would be more appropriate to represent them with a pie chart, which visually demonstrates the values' relation to one another. If the $171.64 instead represented expenditures of a $2,452.00 budget, an easier way to express this relation is with a 7% slice of a pie.

That being said, the rules above mainly focus on general best practices for X,Y graphs: bar charts, line charts, and other graphs with axes. Some of these items apply to other charts, like 3 through 5. To ensure the integrity of your models, you should review the rules for other charts that are available on Excel such as sunburst or whisker plots. Due to the impact of inaccurate investigative modeling, Excel has guides for charts and graphs using wizards. The next sections will cover how to use these wizards for accurate modeling.

Creating Visualizations

In the Q&A, the course asks students to create a bar graph and a demographics table. However, these require variables outside of our focus. For now, we will create a two visualizations comparing the state of Wisconsin and the state of Ohio.

Note:

The slicer has the added benefit of reducing the amount of work needed to generate two separate graphs. This is because the slicer also controls charts and graphs generated using the tables. You can switch between views by toggling the slicer.

---

1. Select the *Avg_Y_Earnings*pivottable

2. Go to *Insert > PivotChart > Column* and select **Clustered Column**

The fields are already propagated for you in the wizard

3. Select **OK**

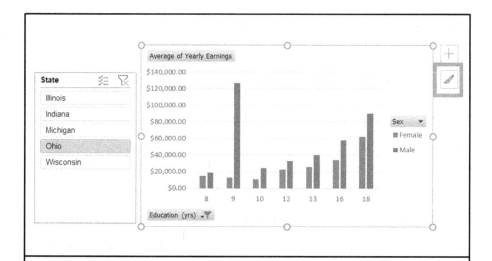

Target: Ohio Bar Graph

This screenshot depicts the Pivot Chart generated after the listed steps. It can be toggled between any of the five listed states with the slicer depicted alongside. Selecting the paintbrush allows you to modify the appearance of the chart. The plus sign lets you toggle the various chart elements on and off such as different axises, their titles, and even including a trend line. The graph can also be isolated along either independent variable (Sex, Education).

4. Save your progress

Interpreting Data using Visualizations

A large part of modeling is reporting on data. In the last chapter we covered modeling as an investigative tool in analysis. Rendering these models accurately can give you visual insight into how and why data behaves. This creates a model so you can analyze the data properly.

However, simply copying and pasting your models for presentation is not enough. To report your findings to others requires additional steps, including arranging models and data in a meaningful way to convey your findings. Many of these steps are dependent on your client, but the majority of these steps involve providing context for your visualizations. This context and composition is important for pointing people to the correct conclusions. Take, for example, our previous example studying the different perspectives of the data broken down by state. By including the State slicer and connecting it to all of the created pivottables, we have created a dynamic dashboard that can be toggled between all 5 states.

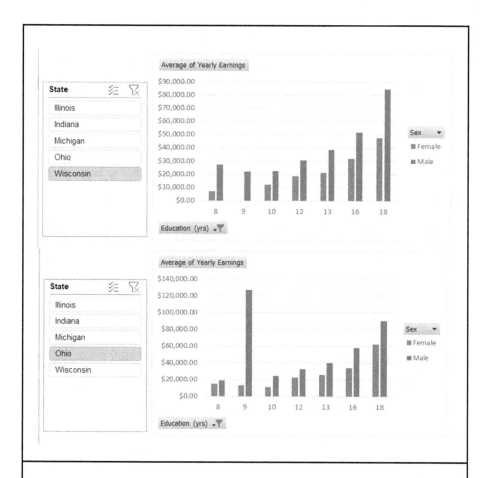

Ohio and Wisconsin Pivot Chart Comparison

These two screenshots are two shots of a dynamic pivot chart broken down by state. Recall our side by side comparison of the Pivottables in an earlier section. Also recall the question about representing the gap in the Wisconsin data. Are they well represented using this bar graph?

In the previous section about analysis we discussed at length the need for "how" and "why" questions to complete analysis. With these detailed charts and graphs, we can easily postulate about why the aspect of the data occurs. For example, one possible question inspired by the Wisconsin pivottable was "Why is there a gap in the data for females with only 9 years of education?" Looking at the total count of data for Wisconsin, one can hypothesize that it is due to the small sample size in comparison with another state like Ohio. Just looking at the total values, Ohio had roughly three times as many females reporting than Wisconsin. Comparing 200 indivuals to 600, that is a difference of about 400 indivuals.

However, looking at the pivottables, it is difficult to make a conclusion about trends. It is only when the data is properly visualized that we can come to some conclusions. Datasets with a small population size tend to have chaotic trends. This is because there are fewer individual data points that could lend themselves to a smooth trend. Therefore, it is difficult to identify a curve or a pattern with smaller population sizes. Going by this reasoning, we would expect that Wisconsin would have no identifiable shapes or trends.

With this hypothesis and comparing it to the actual data, the opposite seems to be true. Wisconsin, despite the lack of females in one of its data points, has a more identifiable shape. The bars form a rolling hill shape indicating a healthy dataset. There may be no data at this datapoint because of how narrowly the chart is broken down. There simply may have been no females with only 9 years of education who reported a salary.

Ohio, in contrast, has one large outlier, particularly at 9 years of education. There could be several reasons for this, including industry trends within Ohio. For example, there could be a large push for high paying positions that don't require a college degree, such as union jobs where people progress to higher pay grades on seniority. Someone who started working earlier and did not attend college would, therefore, make more money in this scenario. The only way to confirm this is through investigative research such as interviews, or looking at additional variables such as age.

One possible approach to research is to get more data. This dataset was originally collected in March 1999. There have been several censuses conducted since then. Further, getting and cleaning the data would be easy with the skills we have practiced. After converting the worksheet to a template, we can generate recorded variables using the formulas already in the sheet. Further, you can build macros to generate pivot tables since the data will be structured in the same way. Finally, you could build dynamic self-service reporting systems through macro, even comparing the different census datasets with one another.

Chapter 6

Troubleshooting

This final chapter will cover troubleshooting scenarios. Thesce solutions are indexed by the scenarios that they address. This chapter will also refer to the associated activity or demonstration, which is good for practicing work arounds.

Power Pivot Ribbon Disappears

Sometimes your Add-ins may disappear if Excel restarts itself. To restore the Power Pivot Ribbon in your main menu, follow this step by step solution from Microsoft ("Start the Power Pivot add-in for Excel," n.d.).

Scenario 1: Power Pivot Ribbon Disappears

1. Go to *File* > *Options* > *Add – Ins*.

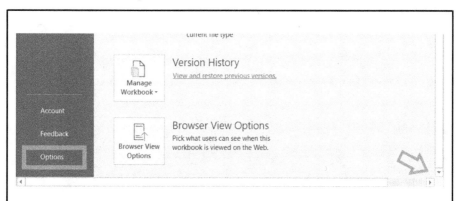

"Options" Location

Be sure to scroll down the Excel: File screen to access the File>Options screen. The Excel: File main screen was designed to be an aggregate of information, therefore, there is a lot of information here about the file and other files on your computer in some cases. This can make it difficult to find the information you need.

You will have to scroll down and navigate to the Options button to access the options window.

2. In the Manage drop-down menu, click **Disabled Items** > **Go**.

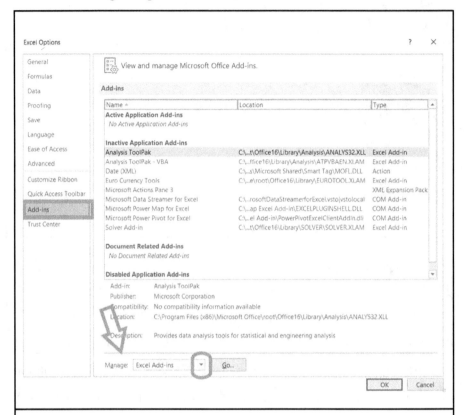

"Add-ins" Dialogue Window

Clicking "Options" will close the Excel: File window and open a separate dialogue window entitled "Excel Options". To access the Excel Options: Add-ins window, you must navigate the menu to the left. The "Manage" box is a drop-down menu at the bottom of the dialogue window. This image shows what appears in the Manage drop-down menu upon opening the window. Click the downward triangle (▼) box to navigate to **Disabled Items**.

3. Select Microsoft Office Power Pivot and then click Enable.

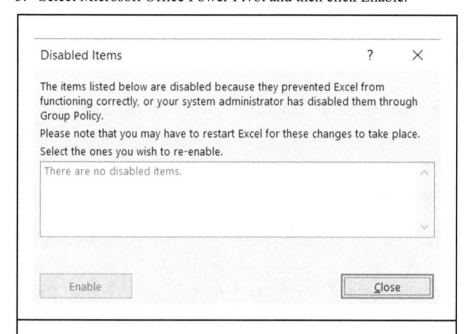

Disabled Items   ?   ✕

The items listed below are disabled because they prevented Excel from
functioning correctly, or your system administrator has disabled them through
Group Policy.
Please note that you may have to restart Excel for these changes to take place.
Select the ones you wish to re-enable.

There are no disabled items.

Enable   Close

Disabled Items Dialogue Box

Clicking "OK" will prompt the Disabled Items Box. If Power Pivot
was disabled it will appear in this menu. If Power Pivot isn't here, it
is enabled, but it still isn't showing in the main menu, then proceed
to the next scenario.

Scenario 2: Ribbon is not restored or disappears from Excel after Enabling Power Pivot

Note:

This solution requires edits to the system Registry. Many outfits require administrative privileges to edit the Registry, since it can affect your computer's entire operating system. You may have to get your office admin to use this solution.

If you have the privileges to make the edits yourself, *take caution!* Do not make any changes to the Registry without creating a restoration point first! This can be done through ("How to Create a System Restore Point in Windows 7," n.d.):

1. *St1art > Control Panel > System and Security*

2. Click on the *System Protection* link

3. In the "System Protection" Dialogue box, click the *System Protection*tab

4. Click on *Create* button and follow the prompts

If the Power Pivot ribbon still doesn't appear, you will have to access the Registry Editor and make changes there. Follow these steps ("Start the Power Pivot add-in for Excel," n.d.):

1. Close Excel and go to *Start > Run*, type in "regegit".

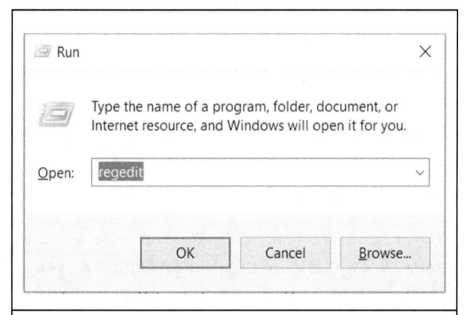

Run Dialogue Box

Going to *Start > Run* brings up the depicted small dialogue box. The Run dialogue box allows you to execute programs using their file name. This dialogue box can also be called using this keyboard shortcut: $[Windows - Key] + [R]$. Type in "regedit" and click okay to access Windows' Registry Editor.

2. Copy: *Computer\HKEY_CURRENT_USER\Software\ Microsoft\Office\ [...]*

   [...]*16.0\User Settings\PowerPivotExcelAddin* into the address bar at the top of the Registry Editor. Be sure that there are no ellipses. "[...]"

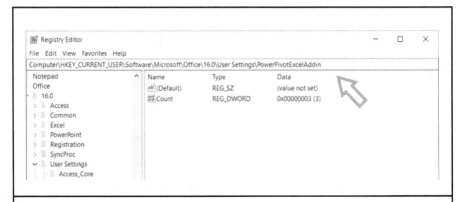

Registry Editor Window: "...\User Settings\PowerPivotExcelAddin..."

Depicts the contents of the ...\User Settings\PowerPivotExcelAddin Folder. You can either navigate to ***HKEY_CURRENT_USER > Software > Microsoft > Office > 16.0 > User Settings***or you can copy in the root address depicted in the address bar. If you choose to copy in the root, the Register Key is case sensitive. The root must be copied verbatim.

3. On the folder navigation menu on the left hand side, **PowerPivotExcelAddin** folder should be highlighted. *Mouse: Right − Click > Delete* the folder.

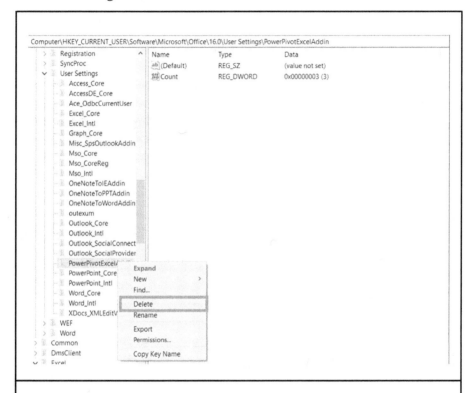

Registry Editor Window Navigation: "...\User Settings\PowerPivotExcelAddin..."

Depicts the folder navigation menu on the left-hand side of the Registry Editor window. Whether you pasted the root or navigated to the folder, this screenshot illustrates your target in the Registry Editor window.

4. Copy: *Computer\HKEY_CURRENT_USER\Software*
   Microsoft\Office\Excel\ [...]
   [...]Addins\PowerPivotExcelClientAddIn.NativeEntry.1
   into the address bar at the top of the Registry Editor. Be sure that there are no spaces.

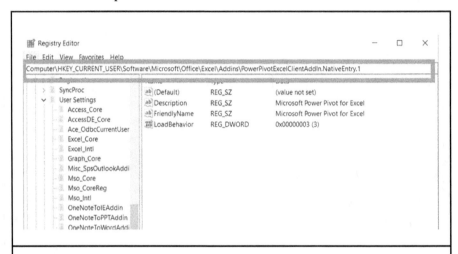

Registry Editor Window:

"...\Addins\PowerPivotExcelClientAddin..."

Depicts the contents of the

...\Addins\PowerPivotExcelClientAddin.NativeEntry.1 Folder. You can either navigate to **HKEY_CURRENT_USER >**
Software > Microsoft > Office > Excel > Addins or you can copy in the root address depicted in the address bar. If you choose to copy in the root, the Register Key is case sensitive. The root must be copied verbatim.

5. On the folder navigation menu on the left hand side, the **PowerPivotExcelClientAddIn.NativeEntry.1** folder should be highlighted. *Mouse: Right − Click > Delete* the folder.

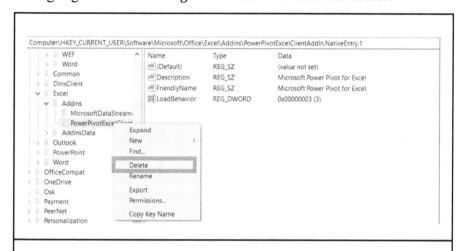

Registry Editor Window Navigation: "...\Addins\PowerPivotExcelClientAddin..."

Depicts the folder navigation menu on the left-hand side of the Registry Editor window. Whether you pasted the root or navigated to the folder, this screenshot illustrates your target in the Registry Editor window.

6. Close the Registry Editor

After completing these steps you have reset the Power Pivot Add-in on Excel. You have reinitialize as if it is a brand new install. Return to the demonstration in chapter 2 and redo the steps to gain access to the Power Pivot Add-in.

Problems with Adding Slicers

The Slicers is an Office 365 Excel 2019 feature that allows you to dynamically change the data. We covered how to deploy them in chapter about analysis in the "Creating: Discovering and validating new perspectives on the data" section. This troubleshooting section will cover problems with adding slicers.

Scenario 1: Slicer button is Inactive

Recall from chapter 1 that all modern Excel products are controlled by their licenses. For those who have a subscription service, their subscription controls what features their build of Excel will allow them to have. This same subscription based service also monitors the types of files opened on Excel. While you can open and operate an older Excel file in Office 365 Excel 2019, that file will be placed in compatibility mode to ensure the best experience. As an effect, files in compatibility mode won't have access to some features. One of those features is the advanced slicer and filter features.

To gain access to the slicer feature your file must not be in compatibility mode. Here are the steps for getting your file out of compatibility mode:

1. Go to *File* > *Info* and click on **Convert**

File>Info: Compatibility Mode

This screenshot depicts the default window that populates when you select File. This view only happens when your file is in compatibility mode. Older Excel files are placed in compatibility mode to improve performance. However, this can prevent you from using new Office 365 Excel 2019 features such as the improved slicers. Our example file was generated on an older build of Excel, therefore, it was automatically placed in compatibility mode.

2. Go back to your pivottable and you should have access to slicers.

If you still don't have slicers enabled, revisit the conditions for using slicers. For your convenience, the 4 conditions were:

1. You need to be on a desktop build of Excel

2. PivotTables need to be enabled

3. The data must be in a PivotTable

4. Must not be in compatible mode

Finally, ensure that you are engaging with a table or a pivottable. Excel spreadsheets themselves are not tables but just cells with data. Tables, and subsequently pivottables, are a recognized object within Excel.

Scenario 2: Existing Connections Dialogue Box

This dialogue box may pop up after going to *Insert > Filters > Slicer* or while you are trying to segment your pivottables.

Existing Connections Dialogue Box

Screenshot of the dialogue box that propagates when no table or pivot table is selected. This is a verbose error that is trying to communicate a lack of a target.

This error occurs when no table or pivottable is targeted. The solution is to close the window and select a pivot table or table.

Conclusion

This text follows the logical steps from getting started to finalizing a report. First and foremost, you must consider Excel versions and compatibility. This often makes the difference between a freelance data entry and consulting analyst position. Excel files are backwards compatible, meaning that newer builds of Excel will always be able to execute older Excel files. However, Microsoft uses a forwards incompatibility model, and older perpetual licenses are not able to execute newer Excel files. This is important because your client will not be able to review the delivered pivot tables embedded in an Office 365 Excel 2019 file on their old perpetual licensed build. One immediate work around is to present your build on Excel for the web, which is capable of displaying all Excel 2019 features.

This text also overviewed the new Office 365 Excel 2019 functions, which were engineered to reduce expression complexity. These conditional statements and decision based switching functions add a powerful tool for automation outside of VBA. Deploying these functions in pivottables also make the Excel for the web work around more feasible, since Excel for web does not have access to macro ("Work with VBA macros in Excel for the web," n.d.). It is also good since many corporate outfits either limit or ban the use of macro-enabled files for security. Learning how to create macros in VBA is still an excellent "Excel power-user" skill, since it saves time in research and development outfits where macro enabled files are more tolerated. Using modular macros that handle repetitive analytical and report generating tasks is the best practice for using macros. Having one dedicated macro enabled machine for creating reports is also best practice for security in your own outfit.

We also overviewed the analysis process for large datasets, which includes investigative modeling. Of course, the approach of modeling will depend on the nature of the data, but the analysis process is universal for all projects using pivot tables:

1. Making more intelligible views of large data sets through aggregation into pivottables

2. Using modeling to investigate how the data trends and postulate why it trends with several views of the data

3. Creating new perspectives of viewing the data informed by trends and educated ascertations

Finally, we discussed best practices for reporting data and Excel features that assist with implementing these best practices. Many wizards and prompts in Excel have best practices built in, such as labeling and improved text handling using $TEXTJOIN()$ in Office 365 Excel 2019. Throughout the text, we have shared notes about Excel feature compatibility and workarounds for presenting Excel files in dated perpetual outfits. In general, data and reports can be viewed in Excel for the web. A desktop build of Excel is required to edit pivottables and reports.

Beyond specific "Power User skills," the most important aspect to take away from this text is the Power User mindset: how to use a feature to achieve some specific goal. Remember that there is a difference between features and how to use them, and the *functionality* of a feature. Excel and its pivottables are merely a tool for extracting potentially decision informing insights from large datasets.

People tend to overlook the creative aspects of data analysis, since "creativity" is usually associated with some abstract, boundless activity reserved for people in the artistic field. Even artists have to practice techniques to properly render and represent ideas that inform culture. It takes a similar methodical approach to be truly successful and insightful in research settings as well. Your presentations must answer why this dataset matters and how it will impact your client's bottom line.

Most importantly, data analysts must have integrity. We discussed scientific integrity, and models that follow the basic principles in data modeling are considered to be scientifically sound. Those that do not follow the principles can be due to human error, which is why Microsoft has wizards that mitigate this risk. However, individuals who make a deliberate choice to modify their models to support their beliefs lack professional integrity. There may be times when peers or even your superiors will ask for models that affirm their efforts in sales, outreach, or other items. It is always best to be truthful and provide an accurate reflection of the data to maintain not only your integrity, but the integrity of the data analysis field.

Reference

Bar graph missing zero1—Misleading graph—Wikipedia. (n.d.).
Retrieved August 26, 2019, from
https://en.wikipedia.org/wiki/Misleading_graph#/media/File:Ba
r_graph_missing_zero1.svg

Consolidate multiple data sources in a PivotTable. (n.d.). Retrieved
August 27, 2019, from https://support.office.com/en-
us/article/consolidate-multiple-data-sources-in-a-pivottable-
8f476919-40b3-4133-9870-26f4d9f21ad6

Create a PivotTable to analyze worksheet data. (n.d.). Retrieved
August 20, 2019, from https://support.office.com/en-
us/article/create-a-pivottable-to-analyze-worksheet-data-
a9a84538-bfe9-40a9-a8e9-f99134456576

File:Example truncated bar graph.svg—Wikimedia Commons. (n.d.).
Retrieved August 26, 2019, from
https://commons.wikimedia.org/wiki/File:Example_truncated_
bar_graph.svg

File:Scatter Plot with missing categories.svg—Wikimedia Commons.
(n.d.). Retrieved August 26, 2019, from
https://commons.wikimedia.org/wiki/File:Scatter_Plot_with_mi
ssing_categories.svg

FORECAST.ETS.STAT function. (n.d.). Retrieved August 24, 2019,
from https://support.office.com/en-us/article/forecast-ets-stat-
function-60f2ae14-d0cf-465e-9736-625ccaaa60b4

Forecasting functions (reference). (n.d.). Retrieved August 24, 2019, from https://support.office.com/en-us/article/forecasting-functions-reference-897a2fe9-6595-4680-a0b0-93e0308d5f6e

How to Create a System Restore Point in Windows 7. (n.d.). Retrieved August 23, 2019, from Dummies website: https://www.dummies.com/computers/operating-systems/windows-7/how-to-create-a-system-restore-point-in-windows-7/

IFS function. (n.d.). Retrieved August 27, 2019, from https://support.office.com/en-us/article/ifs-function-36329a26-37b2-467c-972b-4a39bd951d45

Introductory Econometrics Chapter 3: Pivot Tables. (n.d.). Retrieved August 23, 2019, from http://www3.wabash.edu/econometrics/EconometricsBook/chap3.htm

Keyboard shortcuts in Excel. (n.d.). Retrieved August 27, 2019, from https://support.office.com/en-us/article/keyboard-shortcuts-in-excel-1798d9d5-842a-42b8-9c99-9b7213f0040f

Koble, M. (n.d.). What Is the Life Span of the Average PC? | Chron.com. Retrieved August 20, 2019, from https://smallbusiness.chron.com/life-span-average-pc-69823.html

Microsoft wants you to beta test upcoming Office products and services | Windows Central. (n.d.). Retrieved August 27, 2019, from https://www.windowscentral.com/microsoft-wants-you-beta-test-upcoming-office-products-and-services

Power Pivot keyboard shortcuts and accessibility—Office Support. (n.d.). Retrieved August 26, 2019, from https://support.office.com/en-us/article/Power-Pivot-keyboard-shortcuts-and-accessibility-C87D45F9-FFB3-4BA9-AEB0-687627A2B9FF

Start the Power Pivot add-in for Excel. (n.d.). Retrieved August 23, 2019, from https://support.office.com/en-us/article/start-the-power-pivot-add-in-for-excel-a891a66d-36e3-43fc-81e8-fc4798f39ea8

SWITCH function. (n.d.). Retrieved August 27, 2019, from https://support.office.com/en-us/article/switch-function-47ab33c0-28ce-4530-8a45-d532ec4aa25e

The VBA Guide To Excel Pivot Tables. (n.d.). Retrieved August 20, 2019, from The Spreadsheet Guru website: https://www.thespreadsheetguru.com/blog/2014/9/27/vba-guide-excel-pivot-tables

Use slicers to filter data—Office Support. (n.d.). Retrieved August 26, 2019, from https://support.office.com/en-us/article/use-slicers-to-filter-data-249f966b-a9d5-4b0f-b31a-12651785d29d

Where is Power Pivot? (n.d.). Retrieved August 23, 2019, from
https://support.office.com/en-us/article/where-is-power-pivot-
aa64e217-4b6e-410b-8337-20b87e1c2a4b

Work with VBA macros in Excel for the web. (n.d.). Retrieved August
23, 2019, from https://support.office.com/en-gb/article/work-
with-vba-macros-in-excel-for-the-web-98784ad0-898c-43aa-
a1da-4f0fb5014343

XlConsolidationFunction enumeration (Excel) | Microsoft Docs. (n.d.).
Retrieved August 26, 2019, from
https://docs.microsoft.com/en-
us/office/vba/api/excel.xlconsolidationfunction